Humanity's Paradox

A BELIEVER

ISBN 978-1-957582-14-6 (paperback)
ISBN 978-1-957582-15-3 (eBook)

Copyright © 2022 by A Believer

All rights reserved. No part of this publication may be reproduced, distributed, or transmitted in any form or by any means, including photocopying, recording, or other electronic or mechanical methods without the prior written permission of the publisher.

Printed in the United States of America

Chapter 1

Spiritual Horizon

The last grains of sand are about to expire from the hour glass of life. Have you ever considered, "What is the purpose of life?"

Before the foundation of the world, there was the downfall of the angels. The struggle between 'Good' and 'Evil' begins. By the Grace of God, each of us are given the gift of life and we are created in His Image. Our total being of heart, mind and soul is to lead each of us to the very quintessence of life. A mind to understand God's Word, a heart to discern His Will, a soul and spirit to persevere in faith to our eternal life. No one except God knows the last hour of time. Not even His beloved Son. But one person was given the revelation of the end of time so God's Son can come in glory to judge both the living and the dead.

A Believer

Whoever has ears ought to hear what the Spirit says to the churches. The one with a sharp two-edged sword says this:

> "I know that you live where Satan's throne is, and yet you hold fast to my name and have not denied your faith in me, not even in the days of Antipas, my faithful witness, who was martyred among you, where Satan lives." Rev 2:13

Life is a precious gift, but too many people are all thumbs with the wrappings, lose their way and flounder in a tumultuous, faithless world. For each of us were created in His Image and as a total being were given a heart to love, bear and be resilient; also, a mind to learn the will of the Almighty God and a soul to believe and listen for His call!

The waves were unseasonably rough, the winds howled like coyotes at night and the sails fluttered to the detriment of a poor day to catch any fish. John lost his balance as the boat tossed about. It would take time to season his sea legs to stand firm as he was thrown against the rail of the boat and nearly fell overboard, if it wasn't for the sturdy arms of his older brother. James expeditiously grabbed him and fastened him with cordage to the mast of the boat. Following in the footsteps of their dad, they became fishermen and enjoyed the daily zeal of the catch. Brothers have a special bond and apropos, sisters do to, which magnifies family's love.

Life is a sinuous gauntlet of choices from the daily challenges of the mental, emotional, physical and most importantly the spiritual milieu that we live in. We turn, spin and are tossed about and must acquire the resilience of life in our heart, mind and soul. John learned from his dad and older brother how to navigate some of the challenges of life but how does one survive the vicissitudes of life beyond our control? John groped for the answers to life that no one could adequately explain. How about you? Do you ponder for answers about the hereafter?

Then one day a stranger emerged from the desert clad in a camel's hair garment and walked through their town. He was like no other man that John had ever known. His simple diet consisted of locusts and wild honey and he spoke words that enlivened John's heart like an erupting volcano. John thought to himself, "who is this man?"

He followed him from a distance and listened attentively to his every word that inspired many of the local residence. He spoke to all levels of society and his message was simple, "God's message on the world was imminent, come, repent your sins, be baptized with water and bear fruit for His coming!"

And this is where our story begins!

A Believer

> "Zion shall be redeemed by judgement,
> and her repentant ones by justice.
> Rebels and sinners alike shall be crushed,
> those who desert the Lord shall be consumed.
> You shall be ashamed of the
> terebinths which you prized,
> and blush for the groves which you chose.
> You shall become like a tree with falling leaves,
> like a garden that has no water.
> The strong man shall turn to tow,
> and his work shall become a spark;
> Both shall burn together,
> and there shall be none to quench
> the flames." Is 1:27-31

A new day is dawning and the Zebedee's were rising early as the dad stoked the fire so his wife, Salome, could make breakfast. He called to his sons, James and John, "Top of the morning boy's, rise, shine and give thanks to God, for today should be a fortuitous day to haul a good catch."

The Sea of Galilee also known as Lake Tiberias, contained multiple species of fish but the three primary types that the locals enjoyed and are commercially profitable were the binny which had barbs at the corners of the mouth; the musht, a Tilapia which means "comb" in Arabic, because the fish displays comb-like dorsal fin and finally the Kinneret sardine which resembles a small herring.

It was a six-mile journey from their hometown of Bethsaida to Capernaum where the Zebedee's kept their fishing boat. Due to the Jordan River emptying into the lake, this caused a delta of sediment and a poor area to keep a boat. The sun was rising and it was a pleasurable walk as the dad asked each boy questions from the Torah. John always enjoyed the lessons but his brother, James, struggled with the answers of who, what, where, when, why and how! James was more concerned with fishing and the joys of daily life but John being more tenuous, was always considering the ethereal aspects of life. Sometimes John's spontaneous questions flustered his older brother as he would ask,

"Father, are all angels' intermediaries between God and humanity and what is there assigned duties?"

James would just look at his brother, throw up his arms and roll his eyes at his dad. The father with understanding patience would smile and tell John, "That is an excellent question son, not for me, but for one of the morahs," which is a rabbi in the Judaic faith. Zebedee loved both of his sons, the practical one and the meticulous one that was more contemplative.

Zebedee reminded his sons to remember the words of the prophets, especially Isaiah who saw the truth,

> "Seek the Lord while he may be found,
> call him while he is near.
> Let the scoundrel forsake his way,

> and the wicked man his thoughts;
> Let him turn to the Lord for mercy;
> to our God, who is generous in forgiving.
> For my thoughts are not your thoughts,
> nor are your ways my ways, says the Lord.
> As high as the heavens are above the earth,
> so high are my ways above your ways
> and my thoughts above your thoughts." Is 55:6-9

It was an era where dads scrutinized the teaching of their religious faith on the Word of God and passed on the family trade to their sons to prepare the way of their future. Little did Zebedee know then that the future held a different course for both of his sons. Their boat was moored along the dock where Simon and Andrew kept their fishing trawler. These ancient Galilee boats were 27 feet (8.27 meters) long, 7.5 feet (2.3 meters) wide and a draft height of only 4.3 feet (1.3 meters) for easy hauling in their nets.

The lake with its immediate surrounds has been recognized throughout history for two distinct but beautiful characteristics, first, a sanctuary for the many beautiful birds of black francolins, marbled teals, crested grebes, grey herons and black-headed gulls. And secondly, the miracles of Jesus in faith healings, exorcisms, resurrection and the control over nature, especially with the walking on water.

It isn't a very large lake in comparison to other large bodies of water but earned its place in history due one man, the Son of God! The lake is about 13 miles long, 8 miles wide and the deepest depth of 141 feet. Zebedee scrupulously scoured the skies every evening and morning for the familiar signs of 'red at night, sailors delight' and 'red in the morning, sailors take warning.' He painstakingly took the time to instruct his sons in navigation of dead reckoning or calculating the current position of some moving object by using a fix on some previously determined position and then incorporated estimations of speed, heading direction and time to determine a designation along the lake. For you see, even though the lake was only eight miles wide, a tall figured man standing upright in his boat could see no further then 3.3 or possibly 4 miles if he balanced on his toes. John picked up the crude compass that was in their boat and filled the bowl with water. Their compass consisted of a small bowl of water with a piece of lodestone, a naturally magnetized ore of iron to point in the direction of due north.

The day was balmy and the skies were clear that led to a gigantic day of a good catch. The nets bulged with a haul that took all three to heave and pull hard that tested their muscle power to the brink.

Gasping for air, John gave a mighty sigh as the last haul was pulled aboard. Rubbing his sore muscles, he said to his dad, "I'm glad that was the last load!" James exclaimed, "I agree with you, my brother! Then turned to his dad to get the nod to head in the direction of home. Pulling the halyard to hoist the sail, the boat glided across the surface of the water to reach maximum knots and this was a time of sheer enjoyment as the dad took control of the tiller. This was an exhilarating time as James unlatched a line from the mast and swung out over the surface of the water. The boat, even with a heavy load, glided over the waters as strong winds caught the sails propelling the boat towards home. John joined in the fun as he grabbed for another line and jumped overboard hanging on for dear life. Both were dragged like caught fish through the wake of the boat and enjoyed every exhilarating moment.

Adolescence, that transitional time of physical and psychological development that either could be exhilarating, disappointing or a wake-up call to expand your horizons. James and John were growing, learning and developing exponentially at different expectations that no one could predict. They came ashore, tied up their boat and the two sons helped their dad to offload their catch of the day to market. The dad taught the boys that as the unloading of the catch took place, inspect the boat for any damage. James noticed that the upper gunwales which is the top part of the boat was damaged in a few areas from the heavy hauls of the nets and ropes. Badly needed supplies to make the necessary repairs would have to be purchased before going out to sea again. The sons took the daily catch to market as their dad went to purchase the hardware at the emporium.

It was a time when the rulers of Galilee and the Perea region would levy high revenues on all products to support their lavish life styles. Zebedee rubbed his brow wondering if he could afford the two hundred talents per hundred weights. Lebanese cedar planks along with some oak pegs and bitumen pitch added up to a heavy load and cost.

The Hebrew word for town is Kfar and Capernaum was a fairly large town during the time of Jesus. This is the very town where Jesus called a few young men to follow him and become his first apostles. The town was large enough to have a tax station, infact one of the first apostles was a tax collector. Like all large towns or cities, it was a harbinger of good and evil experiences. Capernaum offered opportunities to work in the grain mills, fishing to fill the market tables and market fairs to sell their artisan trades. But also, large towns were a collective pot for the typical den of thieves, prostitute's and scoundrels that wanted either your money, your virtue or your life!

The scales were loaded both at the fish market and the hardware emporium. A daily good catch out-weighed by a bit the scales at the emporium. Supplies could be purchased and repairs made before going out to sea again. The supplies of Lebanese cedar, oak pegs and some bitumen-pitch were taken to the boat. Three days later and the repairs just about completed to shape the wood, carve the mortise-and-tenon joints and smear the pitch on the boat; all three of the Zebedee's while working, heard a deep voice exclaiming, "Repent, for the kingdom of heaven is at hand!"

It was of him that the prophet Isaiah had spoken when he said: 'A voice of one crying out in the desert,' "Prepare the way of the Lord, make straight his paths."

This time the words penetrated the very souls of both James and John as this stranger continued to preach, "He who is coming after me is mightier than I. I baptize you with water; He will baptize you with the Holy Spirit and with fire."

It was as if their hearts were on fire for each of them burned with zeal and couldn't help but wanted to follow this prophet to a place along the Jordan River. Poor old Zebedee felt left in a dilemma and didn't know what to do next! For both of his sons were on a spiritual horizon to seek, to serve and be ignited into something that was bigger then the both of them! A reawakening, a rebirth was about to take place. Due to their youth, both boy's hearts weren't tarnished from life, their minds were open to the Word of God and their souls enkindled to seek and listen.

This stranger who was about to become known as John the Baptist, was born somewhere in Judaea to Elizabeth, a relative of Mary, the mother of Jesus. His dad was Zechariah, a priest of the order of Abijah. During his formative years in the Judaean desert, he learned from the Essenes, a monastic community about prayer, contemplation and the Word and very Will of God. For from the beginning of time, God chose John to be a voice from the wilderness to prepare the way for His only begotten Son. He grew strong in stature and perceived the capriciousness of people that never could keep a straight path. Most people were like the weather, unpredictable and always changing.

After a transitional period in the desert, John like a thunderbolt, initiated his public ministry, baptizing people in the Jordan River at a place call Bethany beyond the Jordan. Much different from the village of Bethany, where Jesus in due time would visit the siblings of Mary, Martha and their brother Lazarus. Bethany beyond the Jordan, referred to as Bethabara was a small town on the eastern banks of the Jordan River. Just as the river runs through Israel as an important source for watering a parched land, it also runs through the Bible with an even greater supernatural significance. Along the stream can be found a rich, lush riparian vegetation and a diverse array of oak, terebinth, mastic, along with almond and walnut trees. Sandy shores and steep, rocky banks, the river is fairly narrow and easy to cross in most places. Strategically, an excellent place for John the Baptist to minister to the high volume of travelers coming and going.

This is where John and James followed the Baptist to learn more about how to prepare for God's judgement

A Believer

and meet other followers of John. John the Baptist's ethical call for justice and charity required righteousness from all of his followers. Upon the boys leaving their dad Zebedee, he bid them farewell with the words of blessings from the first psalm,

> "Happy those who do not follow
> the counsel of the wicked,
> nor go the way of sinners,
> nor sit with company with scoffers.
> Rather, the law of the Lord is their joy;
> God's law they study day and night.
> They are like a tree planted near streams of water,
> that yields its fruit in season;
> Its leaves never wither; whatever they do prospers."

Zebedee knew all too well, that where ever a person's true heart is; they shall follow their passion! James and John learned well from the ways of the Baptist, for at that time Jerusalem, all Judea, and the whole region around the Jordan were going out to him and were being baptized by him in the Jordan River as they acknowledged their sins. When the Baptist saw many of the Pharisees and Sadducees coming to his baptism, he said to them, "You brood of vipers! Who warned you to flee from the coming wrath?" Mt 3:7-8

Both James and John were amazed at the threatening words addressed to the religious with such jurisdiction that they admired the clout displayed by John.

The Jordan is a unique river where many such miraculous events occurred throughout history. This is especially true of the stretch near Jericho where three important turning points in Israel's history occurred. The significant leadership transitions, of Moses to Joshua, Elijah to Elisha and John the Baptist to Jesus. God's divine calling! For the very baptism of Jesus Christ by John the Baptist took place in the Jordan River, just a few miles north of the Dead Sea and roughly six miles east of Jericho. And as soon as Jesus was baptized, he went up out of the water. At that moment the clouds were parted, heaven was opened, and he saw the Spirit of God descending like a dove and alighting on him. And a voice from heaven said, 'This is my Son, whom I love; with him I am well pleased.' Mt 3:16-17

The Presence of God was revealed at Jesus 'baptism, just as the Presence of God was revealed on Mt. Sini to Moses. Enigmas are more easily accepted then explained. Once Jesus stepped out of the Jordan River, then he was led by the Spirit into the desert to be tempted by the devil. Jesus fasted for forty days and forty nights, and afterwards was hungry. Then the sinister devil tempted Jesus not once, not twice, but three times. Three times the devil deceived and flaunted before Almighty God to trick Jesus to prostrate and worship Satan, the king of all

A Believer

betrayers. But, at this Jesus said to him, "Get away, Satan! It is written: 'The Lord, your God, shall you worship and him alone shall you serve.'" This is a paradox for Satin, that God is always in control!

Picture from Creative Commons

This became the beginning of the Galilean Ministry and the arrest of poor John the Baptist. The inception of being disciples for John the Baptist didn't last long for James and John. They were inspired by his preaching and proclamations! Where does one turn or go? They now walked in the footsteps of despair and being despondent, returned home to their father.

Then one day Jesus was walking along the shore by the Sea of Galilee and noticed two brothers, Simon who is called Peter, and his brother Andrew, casting a net into the sea; they were fishermen by their trade. Now this Jesus who is the only begotten Son of the Almighty God has a divine gift that no other has received. That precious attribute is the ability to read the hearts of all! Jesus could see into the hearts of Simon Peter and Andrew and told them to come after me, and I will make you fishers of men. At this beckoning, they left their nets and followed him.

Then Jesus walked along a little further and saw two other brothers, and that was James and John, Zebedee's sons who had previously followed John the Baptist. Jesus could see the despair in their hearts and feel their despondency. They were in a boat with their father mending the fishing nets. Jesus immediately called to them, and they left the boat and their father. That charismatic nature of Jesus called the first disciples and established the beginning of his ministry to a great multitude of crowds from Galilee, the Decapolis, Jerusalem, Judea and from beyond the Jordan.

The most paramount and ultimate word of God is Jesus Christ! Even though he was in the form of God, did not regard equality with God something to be grasped. Rather, he emptied himself, taking the form of a slave, coming in human likeness; and found human in appearance, he humbled himself, becoming obedient to the point of death, even death on a cross. Because of this, God greatly exalted him and bestowed on him the name which is above every name, that at the name of Jesus every knee should bend, of those in heaven and on earth and even under the earth, and every tongue confess that Jesus Christ is Lord, to the glory of God the Father. Phil 2:6-11

The awesomeness of God before their very eyes, as he talked to the people, not condescending, or pretentious, but to them. The apostles, were inspired, learned and grew in spirit as Jesus taught, healed, cured the ill, the possessed, the paralytics and proclaiming the kingdom of God. His sermons open the spiritual eyes of the multitude of people, as well as his apostles. The youngest of the apostles, John and many of the people's hearts were touched as the Son of God's words penetrated through their souls. There were tears in John's eyes as he realized; this is the Messiah, the Son of God! For He is the full compendium of God's truth, divine mercy and love. God made visible what was invisible through the

Humanity's Paradox

birth of an infant, in all humility, that is the stumbling block for many!

Jesus understood how to captivate the hearts and minds of the multitude of people. He engaged their very heats and souls by instructing the Beatitudes, on how to treat and act towards our neighbor. These simple eight beatitudes illustrate how we should mirror Christ through our attitudes and actions. Then he continues to instruct about our daily lives about anger, the law, adultery, divorce, retaliation and love of enemies. Who ever heard such good news about love of enemies? Are you crazy? This is what agape love from God is all about! Amazement radiated from the crowd. Who is this that speaks of such sublime attributes? Their mundane lives found it difficult to comprehend such lofty ideals?

The apostle John felt for the first time completely contended that indeed, he made the right choice to follow Jesus! John, as well as the other apostles, listened attentively as Jesus continued to explain the spiritual nuances of life, by teaching about the light of the body, dependence on God and answers to their daily prayers.

Jesus looked at the crowd, raised his arms and cried out, "Ask and it will be given to you; seek and you will find; knock and the door will be opened to you."

The apostles contemplated on every word that Jesus said and came to realize that the asking must be reverently, the seeking sincerely, and the knocking continuously to persevere to God. Then Jesus said to them, "Do to others whatever you would have them do to you." This new precept for them is the golden rule of life! As he continued his ministry of preaching, healing and casting out demons, Jesus sought more apostles that had sturdy hearts and devout souls.

It was a conundrum for many when Matthew, the tax collector, is beckoned to join the bona fide group. Infact look at each of the twelve apostle's persona, and as admirable as each were in sincerely seeking to follow Christ, each of them was human and had their failures. Peter who is selected as the rock of whom Jesus will build his church, comes to deny Jesus three times before the cock will crow. Thomas doubts and Judas betrays! Incomprehensible for Judas to see the glory of God and to betray Him. But God's divine mercy is for each of us unfathomable.

The apostles were people just like us, frail, sinners, and stumbling through life, but through Christ overcame life's obstacles and persevered through the many spiritual, physical and mental barriers. All the apostles were attentive when Jesus talked about true discipleship by saying, "Not everyone who says to me, 'Lord, Lord,' will enter the kingdom of heaven, but only the one who does the will of my Father in heaven. He then continued to teach heavenly truths to the disciples but to the multitude of people, he taught in parables.

The disciples approached him and said, "why do you speak to them in parables?"

Jesus replied, "Because knowledge of the mysteries of the kingdom of heaven has been granted to each of you, but to them it has not been granted." This is why I speak to them in parables, because they look but do not see and hear but do not listen or understand. Isaiah's prophecy is fulfilled in them, which says:

> 'Gross is the heart of this people,
> they will hardly hear with their ears,
> lest they see with their eyes and
> hear with their ears and understand
> with their heart and be converted
> and I heal them.'

This is why each of us are cautioned by our Lord – Do not hardened your hearts today! For when the hearts are hardened, the mind closes to the Will of God, and the soul becomes an empty vessel.

John, the youngest of the apostles, listened attentively to every word Jesus spoke and watched admirably as the Son of God cleansed the lepers, healed the sick, the paralytics, the hemorrhaged, the blind, the mute, the deaf and even raised the dead. There was no limit to his compassion and his divine mercy is unfathomable! John observed the tenderness of Jesus and kept all these sentiments within his heart.

Two by two our Lord sent out his disciples throughout the region, Simon called Peter and his brother

A Believer

Andrew; James, the son of Zebedee, and his brother John, the youngest of all the apostles; Philip and Bartholomew, Thomas and Matthew the tax collector; James, the son of Alphaeus, and Thaddeus; Simon the Cananean, and Judas Iscariot who betrayed him.

Christ encouraged all of his disciples by telling them, what I say to you in the darkness, speak in the light; what you hear whispered, proclaim on the housetops. And definitely do not be afraid of those who kill the body but cannot kill the soul; rather, be afraid of the one who can destroy both soul and body in Gehenna.

There were many such fortuitous moments where Jesus taught by example and not by word alone. The walking on water, feeding of the five thousand, the healings at Gennesaret; Jesus understood all too well that it boils down to this, that faith is a belief and trust in God is action. The daily struggle with placing our trust entirely in God is something each of us must face at one point or another in our lives. This is why when the apostles asked Jesus to teach us to pray, he replied,

"Our Father who art in heaven, hallowed be your name'

your kingdom come, your will be done, on earth as in heaven.

Give us today our daily bread; and forgive us our trespasses,

as we forgive those who trespass against us and lead us not into temptation, but deliver us from evil." Amen

Thy will be done and not mine is a stumbling block for many including the beginning apostles who were trying desperately to follow the example of Jesus. John, being extremely concerned for John the Baptist, looked to Jesus for consolation about his first mentor. Jesus smiled and repeated the words, thy will be done! We must believe and trust in God that in His time all things will be made right!

The arrest of John the Baptist was upsetting to the young disciple, but when his death by beheading occurred, this was traumatic for John.

Whenever the apostle's faith was shaken, Jesus would ask pertinent questions to jump-start their faith and inspire them to persevere, for he alone knew all to well the ultimate test of life that was coming. As Jesus turned to his disciples, he asked them, "Who do people say that the Son of Man is?"

Each of them had their own response's by saying, "Some say John the Baptist, others Elijah, and still others Jeremiah or one of the prophets."

He said to them, "But who do you say that I am?"

It was Simon Peter that said in reply, "You are the Messiah, the Son of the living God."

Jesus smiled, and nodded his head and then said, "Blessed are you, son of Jonah. For flesh and blood has not revealed this to you, but my heavenly Father. And so, I say to you, you are Peter, and upon this rock I will build my church, and the gates of the netherworld shall not prevail against it. I will give you the keys to the kingdom of heaven. Whatever you bind on earth shall be bound in heaven; and whatever you lose on earth shall be loosed in heaven."

Where does one begin with the colossal task to build a witness to the kingdom where one does not exist? Through three short years and a monumental imminent three days of passion, this was the mission of Jesus. He began by selecting disciples and setting conditions for that discipleship to build a church and forewarn them through successive predictions to his passion. And like most teachers, the responses from his students weren't always admirable.

For when Jesus began to show his disciples that he must go to Jerusalem and suffer greatly from the elders, the chief priests, and be killed and on the third day be raised. Peter then took him aside and began to rebuke him by saying,

"God forbid, Lord! No such thing shall happen to you."

Jesus turned and said to Peter, "Get behind me, Satan! You are an obstacle to me. You are thinking not as God does, but as human beings do."

These were very harsh words for Peter to comprehend, and he had difficulty in understanding their full significance. As Jesus looked into the eyes of his disciples, he could see desperation in some and hopelessness in others. To dispel their fears, he then said to them, "Whoever wishes to come after me must deny themselves, take up their cross, and follow me. For whoever wishes to save your life will lose it, but whoever loses their life for my sake will find it. For the Son of Man will come with his angels in his Father's glory, and then he will repay everyone according to their conduct."

Each apostle struggled to grasp the meaning of these words, but John, the youngest of the apostles, embraced these words in his heart. And so didn't a few of the other apostles. Jesus quietly observed their reactions and shortly thereafter, he took Peter, James and John and led them up a high mountain by themselves. And he was transfigured before them along with Moses and Elijah to his right and to his left.

Then Peter said to Jesus, "Lord, it is good that we are here."

While Peter was still speaking, behold, a bright cloud cast a shadow over them, then from the cloud came a voice that said, "This is my beloved Son, with whom I am well pleased; listen to him."

When the disciples heard this, they prostrated themselves and were very much afraid. But Jesus understanding their fear, came and touched them, saying, "Rise, and do not be afraid."

And when the disciples raised their eyes, they saw no one else but Jesus alone. As they were coming down the mountain, Jesus charged them, "Do not tell the vision to anyone until the Son of Man has been raised from the dead."

This is mind blowing, heart bursting, soul exploding; that God intervened in their lives to reveal a divine revelation of His Son. This is definitely paramount in the lives of the apostles. God revealed himself to Abraham and the patriarchs, Moses, King David and the prophets and now to the apostles. Who indeed would have the audacity not to listen to God's word? But, one of the apostles would still betray him! How could this possibly happen?

Before the creation of humanity, there was the downfall of the angels. They were in the presence of the Divine, Heavenly Father and yet, were contemptible to do their own will! Because of this, they revolted against God and were hurled out of heaven and do not ever receive redemption! Then God creates humanity and the struggle between good and evil continues from the garden of paradise. Humanity does have redemption which the fallen angels do not have! This is why God sent His Son into the world. God so loved the world, that he sent His only begotten son to be our savior and sacrifice, our sacrificial lamb for redemption, if we only believe, trust and follow Him! What does it mean to follow the Divine Son? God sent his son not only to die for us, but to establish the blueprint to eternal life!

Jesus clearly proclaims that he is the way, the truth and the life; he is the way to eternal truth to eternal life and demonstrates this along his way to Jerusalem. For he performs many more healings and miracles to open the spiritual eyes of the people to soften their hearts, selfish wills, and open their souls to receive God's grace. Why, one may ask; because this was the mission of the only begotten son of God! As they were gathering in Galilee, Jesus said to his apostles, "The Son of Man is to be handled over to authorities, and they will kill him, and he will be raised on the third day."

Baffled and disheartened, all his disciples were overwhelmed with the second prediction of his passion and grieved. They heard the words but their minds could not comprehend the meaning. This was Jesus' way for preparing them for what is coming and then and only then would his disciples understand the true meaning of rise from the dead. Jesus as the true Son of God would overcome sin and death to lead us to new life.

All the apostles grieved, but John kept these predictions within his heart and persevered to become the disciple that Jesus loved. Life is a mystery to be lived, an enigma of spiritual events that are inexplicable except for one thing, God made them possible through the Holy Spirit!

A dichotomy existed within Jesus between the spiritual and the temporal world. How does one adequately prepare those who have not seen the glory of God's Kingdom? Teaching his disciples was difficult at times, especially from some of his disciples' obtuse questions.

Philip said to him, "Master, show us the Father, and that will be enough for us."

Jesus shook his head in disbelief and responded, "Have I been with you for so long a time and you still do not know me, Philip? Whoever has seen me has seen the Father. Do you not believe that I am in the Father and the Father is in me?"

Jesus stopped speaking for a few minutes to allow his words to take root, not only for Philip, but for all the apostles. Then he began speaking again slowly, for his message was to take root in their heart, mind and soul.

"The words that I speak to you, I do not speak to you on my own. The Father who dwells in me is doing his works. Believe me that I am in the Father and the Father is in me, or else believe because of the works themselves."

Jesus again stopped speaking and looked at each of his apostles and then said, "If you love me, you will keep my commandments, and I will ask the Father, and he will give you another Advocate to be with you always, the Spirit of truth, which the world cannot accept, because it neither sees nor knows it. But you will know it, because it remains with you, and will be in you. I will not leave you orphans. I have told you this while I am with you. The Advocate, the Holy Spirit that the Father will send in my name – he will teach you everything and remind you of all that I have told you." He turned and started to walk away but stopped and turned back towards the apostles and said,

"Peace I leave with you; my peace I give to you. Not as the world gives do I give it to you. Do not let your hearts be troubled or afraid. You heard me explain this to you, that I am going away and I will come back to you. If you loved me, you would rejoice that I am going to the Father; for the Father is greater than I. And now I have told you this before it happens, so that when it happens you may believe.

The explanation of the sublime versus the mundane required a forbearance from Jesus that went well beyond the everyday patience of most people. Twelve ordinary men living this temporal existence are called. Called for what? Called by who? Why are they called? Only one could furnish the answers! And he happens to be the Son of God! This is why Jesus is known as the Spiritual Bridge, for he will bring the disciples and us to God. He called and they followed for the yearning was too strong to break. If the heart listens, the soul yearns and the mind takes it's time to catch-up, that is to comprehend. In three short years a conversion took place to prepare them for the Holy Spirit to build a church!

Every time Jesus felt that the disciples were being elevated to the Most-High, they quickly pulled Jesus back to earth with their innuendo's, actions and misconceptions. The local children were brought to Jesus that he might lay his healing, hands on them and pray.

A Believer

The disciples rebuked them, but Jesus said, "Let the children come to me, and do not prevent them; for the kingdom of heaven belongs to such as these." After he placed his hands on them, he went away to pray.

Step by step he walked and step by step they followed and on the way to Jerusalem he unveiled the third prediction. That the Son of Man will be handed over to the chief priests and scribes, and they will condemn him to death. Then they will hand him over to the Roman soldiers to be mocked, scourged and crucified, and he will be raised on the third day.

Again Jesus, as he tried to explain the sublime was pulled back to earth by a request of James and John to be seated at his right and left side in his kingdom. Jesus simply replied, "You do not know what you are asking, can you drink the cup that I am going to drink?" Jesus, along with his disciples, continued their journey and he was moved to pity for two blind men and touched their eyes to heal them. They could see! Now, if only his disciples could see.

When they finally drew near to Jerusalem, in a place called Bethphage, Jesus sent two of his disciples to go into the village and find an ass tethered and a colt with her. The disciples did as Jesus had ordered them. They brought the ass and the colt and laid their cloaks over them, and Jesus sat upon them.

Imagine that, he came into the world born in a stable, humbled beyond all means and his triumphant entry into Jerusalem riding on an ass. The epitome of what it means to be humble, the power, the glory and the divine mercy of Almighty God before their very eyes riding into Jerusalem! The very large crowd spread their cloaks on the road, while others cut branches from the palm trees and strewed them on the road. The crowds preceding him and those following him were jubilant in all exultation crying out,

"Hosanna to the Son of David;
blessed is he who comes in the name of the Lord;
hosanna in the highest."

The whole city was shaken and asked, "Who is this?"

And the crowds replied, "This is Jesus the prophet, from Nazareth in Galilee."

The crowds and the apostles were ecstatic with joy!

He proceeded to the temple area and lo and behold, what did he find? The temple area is supposedly a place for sacrifice, devotion and prayer but instead was used as a bizarre for selling and buying. Jesus in a fit of indignation overturned the tables and drove out all that were engaged in the barter of let's make a deal.

The following day as the disciples trailed behind Jesus, he became hungry and noticed a fig tree on the side of the road. Walking over to the tree, he observed that there was no fruit on the tree. This was the proper moment for a learning lesson for the disciples as Jesus turned to the fig tree and cursed it. No sooner had he done this and the fig tree immediately withered. The disciples were amazed. Jesus explained to his disciples the power of prayer, that whatever you ask for in prayer and do not waver in faith, you will receive.

The power of the walk; no radio, no television, no media, no phones, and definitely no computers, except word by word, through neighbor to neighbor the message of God spread. Jesus taught through many more parables, and the religious questioned his authority and asked him about taxes, the resurrection and which commandment of the law is the greatest? Always being tested by all, his disciples, the people, Satan, the religious authorities, the Pharisees and Sadducees and yes, even His heavenly Father, the Son of God was weary at times.

But he always knew who he is and where he came from and arose to each occasion and simply said, "You shall love the Lord, your God, with all your heart, with all your soul, and with all your mind. This is the greatest and the first commandment. The second is like it: You shall love your neighbor as yourself."

One day as he was sitting on the Mount of Olives, the disciples approached Jesus privately and asked many questions. He wiped his brow, looked up towards heaven and then began to explain the beginning of calamities, the great tribulation and the coming of the Son of Man.

Each explanation led to more questions of when, how and where as he explained,

> "After tribulation the sun will be darkened,
> and the moon will not give its light,
> and the stars will fall from the sky,
> and the powers of the heavens will be shaken.
> And then the sign of the Son of
> Man will appear in heaven,
> and they will see the Son of Man coming
> upon the clouds of heaven with power and great glory.
> And he will send out his angels
> with a trumpet blast, and
> they will gather his elect from the four winds,
> from one end of the heavens to the other."

Chapter 2

Transitions

Life is a precious gift; a path we must all walk from the temporal to the spiritual but we never walk it alone; the choice is ours to accept, believe and follow. From His love, he created us and with His love he will lead us to our heavenly home. That love is Jesus Christ!

The vignettes of the Passion of Christ were instrumental to make transparent the divinity of our Lord; from the Anointing at Bethany, the Passover, to the Crucifixion, Resurrection and Ascension. Each of the apostles learned from his teachings, healings and miracles. Then to the repertoire of his actions comes the passion of the cross. These events thunder the wake-up call of his disciples especially after receiving the gifts of the Holy Spirit. All of the apostles were shaken with the crucified Christ, but from his resurrection, ascension and descent of the Holy Spirit, they became steadfast.

Transitions are never easy for any of us but for the apostles it was mission impossible until the coming of the Holy Spirit. Up to that point all of them except for one, failed miserably. John being the youngest of the disciples knew in his devoted heart that there was no other path to follow but Christ! "For we who live are constantly being delivered over to death for Jesus' sake, so that the life of Jesus also may be manifested in our mortal flesh." 2Cor 4:11

In a place called Bethany on the Mount of Olives, a few miles from Jerusalem, in the house of Simon the leper, Jesus defends a woman's loving action of anointing his head with perfumed oil in view of his impending death and burial as a criminal. Anyone in those days who was deemed a criminal; their body would not be anointed. Many of the disciples were indignant that this fortuitous action by a woman was committed. Through her intuitive instincts, she administered the necessary oil to anoint and prepare Jesus for his upcoming death. One could say that many of the disciples were short-sighted hence, the necessity for the gifts of the Holy Spirit! This was the foible of most of the disciples that Jesus understood, and the Holy Spirit ameliorated to their resolve. The frailties of humanity are also reinforced by the gifts of the Holy Spirit so that each of us can bear fruit and persevere in faith!

Life's trichotomy of body, soul and spirit is an enigma to be lived and a conundrum to understand.

A Believer

Even for the disciples having Christ as their teacher, there were too many baffling questions and not enough time for all of the answers. John spoke to his older brother James, as a sounding board, about many of the teachings from Christ. He also learned to respect Peter's perspective and Christ's objectivity to select Peter as the rock, the foundation for the church. He would talk to Peter about many of the parables that were difficult to unlock the mystery and find the truth. Jesus understood abundantly that the Holy Spirit would unlock many of the mysteries in due time for those who truly sought-after God's kingdom.

Before the feast of the Passover, Jesus knew that his hour had come to pass from this world to his Father. The devil had already induced Judas Iscariot to hand him over to the religious authorities. During supper, fully aware that the Father had put everything into his power and that he had come from God and was returning to God, he arose from the table and took off his outer garments. He took a towel and tied it around his waist. Then he poured water into a basin and began to wash the disciples' feet and dry them with the towel. When he came to Peter, he strongly objected but Jesus gently warned him that unless he washed all the disciples' feet, he would not have any inheritance with him. Jesus is the epitome of a model to follow so that as he did for them, we should do for others! It is difficult to fathom the humility, mercy and service to others, of our Lord, Jesus, as our model to get to heaven.

It was now time for preparation for the Passover meal. Who would have ever thought that one meal could change the lives of so many people? First with the apostles, and then later with the multitude who partake of the body and blood of our Lord. The Last Supper is one of those transitional events that changed everything for eternal life! God so loved the world that he gave us His only begotten Son; His Son gave of himself in body and blood, so that those who believe in him, might have eternal life. Think about that! This is a divine paradigm shift from one covenant to another! It is definitely worth contemplation. He is the way, the truth and the life! John did not understand this fully now, but after the resurrection understood Christ's divinity better then most. Later on, he came to write one of the most powerful Gospel's, as a testimony to the truth and reveals the divine self of Christ in the seven 'I Am" statements spoken by Jesus Christ. Through our Lord and Savior, we have access to the Kingdom of God for he has said,

"I am the resurrection and the life."

A Believer

(left to right: Bartholomew AKA Nathanael,
James-Minor, Andrew, Peter, Judas, John)
(Jesus Christ, Thomas, James-Greater, Philip,
Matthew, Jude AKA Thaddeus, Simon the zealot)
Picture from Creative Commons

The meal that changed the world, where Jesus predicts the betrayal by one of the apostles presents, and foretells that before the next morning, Peter will deny knowing him three times. While at evening meal, Jesus reclined at table with the Twelve. Then he took bread, said the blessing, broke it, and giving it to his disciples said, "Take and eat; this is my body." Then he took a cup, gave thanks, and gave it to them, saying, "Drink from it, all of you, for this is my blood of the new covenant, which will be shed on behalf of many for the forgiveness of sins."

Then Jesus said to all of them, "This night all of you will have your faith in me shaken, for it is written:

> 'I will strike the shepherd,
> and the sheep of the flock will be dispersed;'

but after I have been raised up, I shall go before you to Galilee."

Time was needed for seeking his heavenly Father in prayer for Jesus was weary. The events at the Last Supper had drained Jesus and troubled him. He gathered the apostles to a place called Gethsemane and told his disciples to sit here awhile so he could pray. He took with him Peter and the two sons of Zebedee, and began to feel deep stress and sorrow. He withdrew from them a little further and kneeling, he prayed, "Father, if you are willing, take this cup away from me for the weight of the world was upon him; still, not my will but yours be done." He was in such agony and his prayer so fervent that his perspiration became like drops of blood falling to the ground. And when he returned to the three disciples, he found them asleep. He said to them, "Why are you sleeping? Get up and pray that you may not undergo the test."

It became rather obvious through the various events of Jesus' life, that Peter, James and John became his confidant's. For they were the eyewitnesses of Jesus' transfiguration, the raising of Jairus daughter and at the

A Believer

Garden of Gethsemane during his agony in prayer. These three disciples witness both the glory and darkest trials of our Lord. While Jesus was still explaining some of the circumstances to them, a crowd approached and was led by none other then one of the original disciples, Judas. For Judas approached our Lord and betrayed him with a kiss, which was a pre-arranged signal for the temple guards and elders to arrest Jesus.

The anguish for Jesus continued as he was brought before the musical parley of the chief priest, scribes, and Roman authorities to question, rebuke and revile him. And in the course of events as Jesus had predicted, Peter denied knowing Jesus not once, not twice but three times. The stare from Jesus towards Peter revealed his deep sorrow, and Peter wept bitterly. He vehemently denied, out of fear, the one and only begotten Son of God. And this disciple, Peter, was selected to be the rock for the beginning of the church. This shaky beginning shows the type of precarious grip that satan has on the world.

Jesus was brought before Pontius Pilate, the fifth governor of the Roman province of Judaea, serving under the Emperor Tiberius Caesar. After countless questions and numerous accusations, Pontius Pilate simply did not find Jesus guilty which enflamed the religious leaders. Upon learning that he was a Galilean, Pontius Pilate released Jesus to the custody of Herod who was the ruler of Galilee and the Perea region. Now Herod was a dastardly bastard, a tyrant responsible for the gruesome death of John the Baptist.

Herod was the one that had John arrested and bound in prison, all because of the deceitful woman, Herodias, the wife of his brother Philip. This conceited bigot who desired his brother's wife, married her unlawfully. He definitely possessed the pride of Satan! John the Baptist had personally told Herod, in no uncertain terms, that it was unlawful for him to have his brother's wife. Due to this stern rebuke, Herodias harbored a deep-seated grudge against John that led to a merciless vendetta. She plotted in the recesses of her evil mind to strike back at John and waited for the opportune moment.

The pendulum of life swings between good and evil. The apostle John from the virginity of his youth learned during his innocent years from John the Baptist that to maintain a balance in life one must be in continual prayer. Then as he learned from Jesus how to pray, seek and worship the Heavenly Father, his devotion spiritually matured. No one is ever prepared for the inconceivable vicissitudes of life, especially the evil transgressions that bombards a person broadside. This is exactly what happened to John, the apostle that Jesus loved, and the other apostles. First from the beheading of John the Baptist, and then the sequential events of arrest, trial and crucifixion of Jesus.

The invidious envy and blind jealousy of the religious leaders led to a guilty verdict of Jesus. Something difficult to grasp! Since the Pharisees and Sadducees were well versed in the writings of the Torah and the Prophets, who foretold of the coming of a messiah. Blind rage is a terrible consequence of hardening the heart and clouding the mind and soul; the religious leaders completely missed the boat by not seeing Jesus as the coming Messiah. The civil authorities found Jesus' innocent, but the religious authorities induced them to proclaim him guilty. For when Jesus is brought before the high priest who directly asked him, "Are you the Messiah, the son of the Blessed One?"

Then Jesus answered him, "I am; and 'you will see the Son of Man seated at the right hand of the Power and coming with the clouds of heaven.'" The high priest at once tore his garments and said, "What further need have we of witnesses? You have heard the blasphemy." They all condemned him as deserving to die.

It was now time for the feast and the custom for Pontus Pilate to release a prisoner and give the people a choice to release Jesus, who is proclaimed as King of the Jews, or a well-known criminal for inciting a rebellion. In the eyes of the people, the choice was simple as they all shouted, "Crucify him, Crucify him!" So, Pilate, wishing to satisfy the crowd, released the known criminal to them and, after he had Jesus scourged, handed him over to be crucified.

The tumultuous events that followed were unconscionable for the 'Son of God'! From the mockery by the solders at the Praetorium, the scourging at the pillar, the crowning with thorns, to the carrying of his cross. The 'Walk of Christ', the unfathomable divine mercy for us, to die for our sins, is proof of God's Divine love for us all! Redemption for us, as unfathomable as it may be, Christ became our sacrificial lamb. He gained for us what we could not do for ourselves!

The apostle, John, followed Christ from a distance as he carried his cross. The agony and strain on Jesus caused much stress and discernment for those that truly loved Jesus and followed his hallowed footsteps in silence. Jesus and two other condemned men were taken by the Roman soldiers from the praetorium in Jerusalem to the place of execution known as Golgotha. The very name meant, a place of the skull.

The condemned men usually carried their cross to the place of execution, but Jesus weakened by the severe beatings and scourging at the pillar had fallen for the first time before coming to the city gate. Infact, Jesus fell not once, not twice but three times as the Roman soldiers instructed a passer-by to help carry the cross.

The name of the person who bore the weight of the crossbar was Simon of Cyrene, a city of northern Libya in northern Africa. Cyrene had a large colony of Jews and Simon must have traveled to Jerusalem as a pilgrim to celebrate the feast of Passover.

The narrow streets leading to the place of execution were densely crowded with people jeering and cheering.

A Believer

Many were curious to see a man passing by to his execution. Infact, the very sight of a tortured person on his way to such a cruel death was an intimidation and a deterrent for the many on-lookers. Among this crowd were a group of women who cried out to Jesus in pity and anguish. Jesus urged them, "Daughters of Jerusalem, do not weep for me; weep instead for yourselves and for your children, for indeed, the days are coming when people will say, 'Blessed are the barren, the wombs that never bore and the breasts that never nursed.'

Jesus' own words echo the opening words of Isaiah 54: 'Sing O barren woman who never bore a child.'

Now two others, both criminals, were led away with Jesus to be executed on that first Good Friday. Each were nailed to their crosses with nails that were more like spikes, seven to nine inches long with the girth of a large man's thumb. Excruciating pain burst forth as the nails were hammered into their hands and feet. Three crosses stood on Golgotha. Jesus hung on the middle cross, willing to take the punishment we deserved. On the other crosses hung two thieves, condemned for their own crimes. We never learn the names of the two thieves but from the course of events, it is irrelevant because these two come to represent opposing behaviors. One is arrogant right up to the end; the other is repentant. Every person in life has choices to make. Which will we be, arrogant or humble and penitent? To be truly sorry for our sins requires a lifetime of choices.

Humanity's Paradox

Picture from Creative Commons

One reads the words in Scripture that these men were thieves, robbers and evil doers. Those descriptions give some insight as to why these two men were crucified. Above Jesus, our innocent Lord, there was an inscription that read,

"This is the King of the Jews."

Now one of the criminals hanging there reviled Jesus by saying if you are the Messiah then save yourself and us, to prove that you are the Son of God. The other criminal sternly rebuked him and adamantly told his conspirator that they were justly condemned for their crimes but that this man has done nothing criminal. Then in a moment of repentance, he turned to Jesus and said,

"Jesus, remember me when you come into your kingdom."

Jesus replied, "Amen, I say to you, today you will be with me in Paradise."

What beautiful words to calm the soul!

It was now about noon and darkness came over the whole land until three in the afternoon because of an eclipse of the sun. Then the veil of the temple was torn down the middle. Jesus cried out in a loud voice,

"Father, into your hands I commend my spirit"; and when he had said this, he breathed his last.

The centurion who witnessed what had happened glorified God and said, "This man was innocent beyond doubt."

When all the people who had gathered for this spectacle saw what had happened, they returned home beating their breasts. But all Jesus' acquaintances, including the apostle John, stood at a distance which included the women and Mary, his grieving mother, who had followed him from Galilee and saw these events.

Shaken, rattled and wondering where to turn, John, the youngest of the apostles and the other eleven were stymied as to what to do next! As grief stricken and frightened that the disciples were, they did not attempt to leave Jerusalem and return to their own homes. They all stayed for three days to witness the resurrection of the Messiah. Not only did Jesus' disciples know of the prophecy of His death and resurrection, but the chief priests and Pharisees knew. Knowing that Jesus had promised to arise from the grave was the reason behind

Humanity's Paradox

Jewish authorities beckoning the Roman governor Pilate to have Roman soldiers guard the tomb of Jesus.

Now there was a virtuous and righteous man by the name of Joseph from Arimathea, who was also a disciple of Jesus but in secret, due to fear of the Jews. He went to Pilate and asked for the body of Jesus; and Pilate ordered the body to be handled over to him. Nicodemus also came bringing a mixture of myrrh and aloes along with other spices. They took the deceased body of Jesus and bound it with the burial cloths along with the spices according to the Jewish burial custom. Then they laid him in a rock hewn tomb which no one had yet been buried.

The enigma of the purpose of Christ death can only be accepted in faith. God has given us multiple avenues for our faith; the Soul, Jesus our Lord, the Holy Spirit, the Holy Church, prayer, worship, along with many forms of devotion. Since the Holy Spirit had not descended as yet, the apostles were at a loss for loosing Jesus. Until his resurrection occurs in three days and until the descent of the Holy Spirit on Pentecost, their spirit will then be awakened and consummated.

After the death of our Lord, the apostle John reflected on every word that Jesus spoke to them. He recalled the very words of Jesus as he said, "Enter through the narrow gate; for the gate is wide and the road broad that leads to destruction, and those that enter through it are many. How narrow the gate and constricted the road that leads to life. And those who find it are few."

Mt 7:13-14 And like a thunder bolt that strikes, John understood that Jesus is that gate to eternal life.

Through the ages, God our Heavenly Father, revealed himself to the Patriarchs, established a covenant with Moses for His chosen people; now through Jesus Christ, His only begotten Son, he revealed the divinity in the transfiguration to Peter, James and John and established a new covenant through Jesus at the Last Supper for all whoever partakes of the body and blood of Christ. The blueprint of eternal life is set to unfold and will be established through the Holy Church! The course of actions begins with baptism, signs instituted by Jesus to give us grace from above.

Picture from Creative Commons

On the first day of the week, Mary of Magdala, came to the tomb early in the morning, while it was still dark, and saw the stone removed from the tomb. In haste, she ran to Simon Peter and to the other disciple whom Jesus loved and said to them, "They have taken the Lord from the tomb, and we don't know where they have put him."

So, Peter and the other disciple went out and came to the tomb. They both ran vigorously, but the other disciple ran faster than Peter due to his youth and arrived at the tomb first. He bent down and saw the burial clothes there, but did not venture in. When Simon Peter arrived after the disciple John, he went into the tomb and saw the burial cloths there, and the cloth that had covered his head rolled up in a separate place. Then the disciple John also went in and he saw and believed. For both of the disciples did not yet understand the scripture that he had to rise from the dead. Then the disciples returned home.

But Mary of Magdala stayed outside the tomb weeping. She wept soberly and peered into the tomb and saw two angels to her astonishment in white sitting there, one at the head and one at the feet where the body of Jesus had been. The angels turned and said to her, "Women, why are you weeping?"

She replied to them, "They have taken my Lord, and I don't know where they laid him."

She turned around and saw our Lord standing there, but did not recognize that it was Jesus. He said to her, "Woman, why are you weeping? Whom are you looking for?"

A Believer

Then Jesus called her by name in a consoling manner, "Mary!"

She turned and said to him, "Teacher."

Jesus said to her, "Stop holding on to me, for I have not yet ascended to the Father. But go to my brothers and tell them, 'I am going to my Father and your Father, to my God and your God.'" Then Mary of Magdala went and announced to the disciples that she indeed had seen the risen Lord and repeated what Jesus told her to say.

The very evening of that first day of the week where the disciples were staying, the doors were locked for fear of the Jews. Jesus appeared and stood in their midst and said to them, "Peace be with you." After he had said this, he showed them his hands and his side where the soldier had thrust his lance and immediately flowed blood and water. The disciples rejoiced when they recognized the Lord.

Jesus then again said to them, "Peace be with you. As the Heavenly Father has sent me, so also I send you." And when he had said this, he breathed on them and said, "Receive the Holy Spirit. Whose sins you forgive are forgiven them, and whose sins you retain are retained."

One of the Twelve known as Thomas, also called Didymus, was not with the others when Jesus came. The other disciples told Thomas that they have seen the risen Lord. But Thomas doubted that indeed they had seen the Lord and remarked, "Unless I see the mark of the nails in his hands and put my hand into his side, I will not believe."

Now a week later his disciples were gathered together and this time Thomas was with them. Jesus came, although the doors were locked and stood in their midst. Again, Jesus said, "Peace be with you." Then Jesus turned to Thomas and told him to put his finger and feel the scars in his hands from the nail marks and his side where the lance pierced him and do not be unbelieving, but believe.

Thomas replied to Jesus, "My Lord and my God!"

Jesus said to him, "Have you come to believe because you have seen me? Blessed are those who have not seen and have believed."

Now during this brief time that Jesus had with his disciples, he performed many other signs and wonders so that all may come to believe that Jesus is the Messiah, the Son of God, and that through this belief, all may have life in his name. Jesus as he was with his disciples, turned to Simon Peter and asked three times, "Simon, son of John, do you love me?" And three times Peter replied, "Yes, Lord, you know that I love you and by the third request included, "Lord, you know everything; you know that I love you."

Jesus each time told him to either feed my lambs, tend my sheep and feed my sheep that signified he had chosen Peter to be in charge of the newly established

Church, and then Jesus told all of his disciples where to meet him.

The eleven disciples went to Galilee, to the mountain to which Jesus had ordered them. Then Jesus approached them and said, "All power in heaven and on earth has been given to me. Go therefore, and make disciples of all nations, baptizing them in the name of the Father, and of the Son, and of the Holy Spirit, teaching them to observe all that I have commanded you. And behold, I am with you always, until the end of the age."

Therefore, since universal power belongs to the risen Jesus, he gives the eleven a mission that is universal. From the time of Christ's Resurrection, until his Ascension to heaven, Jesus presented himself alive to his apostles by many proofs after he had suffered, appearing to them during forty days and speaking about the kingdom of God. His magnanimous divinity revealed, his benevolence bestowed; he enjoined them not to depart from Jerusalem, but to wait for "the promise of the Father," "for John baptized with water, but in a few days all of you will be baptized with the Holy Spirit." Jesus further explained to diminish all doubts, for the transparency of their mission. "You will receive power when the Holy Spirit comes upon you, and you will be my witnesses in Jerusalem, Judea, Samaria and to the ends of the earth."

When he had said this, as the disciples were looking on, Jesus was lifted up, and a cloud took him from their sight. As the disciples watched him ascending, each one had their own impression of their master and reflected on the praiseworthy virtues that Jesus taught and the shortcomings that each had to overcome. Especially for John, the apostle that Jesus loved, the deep impressions of Jesus' words now come alive in truth and meaning. For he recalls the words, "Destroy this temple and in three days I will raise it up," the apostle John understands it well of the temple of his body.

Who would have ever thought that the exaltation of the cross is our center of moral attraction for the world? The disciples learned from the very Son of God in the college of divine truth. And for John, he receives it with a faithful soul. Now his thoughts rise to a truer intelligence that will be uplifted once the descent of the Holy Spirit is consummated. What a giant leap forward from the fisherman of yesterday to the evangelist of tomorrow.

All of the disciples returned to Jerusalem from the mount of Olivet, which is near Jerusalem, a sabbath day's journey away. When they entered the city, they went to the upper room where they were staying and devoted themselves with one accord to prayer. During that time Peter stood up in the midst of the brothers which had grown beyond the original twelve. He poignantly explained how scripture had to be fulfilled which the Holy Spirit spoke beforehand through the mouth of David, concerning Judas, who was the traitor that guided those who arrested Jesus. He bought a parcel of land with

A Believer

the wages of iniquity, and falling headlong, he burst open in the middle and all his insides spilled out. This became known to everyone who lived in Jerusalem, so that the parcel of land was called Field of Blood. For it is written in the Book of Psalms:

> 'Let his encampment become desolate,
> and may no one dwell in it.'
> And
> 'May another take his office.'

Therefore, it is necessary that one of the men who accompanied us while still with the Lord and gave witness to his resurrection, be selected. So, two of the followers were proposed, Joseph who was also known as Barsabbas and Matthias. Then they all prayed to seek guidance from the Holy Spirit. Then they cast lots and the lot fell upon Matthias, and he was counted with the original eleven apostles.

When the time for Pentecost was fulfilled, they were all in one place together. And suddenly there came from the sky a noise like a strong driving wind, and it filled the entire house that they occupied. Then there appeared to them tongues as of fire, which parted and came to rest on each one of them. And they were all filled with the Holy Spirit.

Many signs and wonders were done among the people at the hands of the apostles. The word of God continued to spread and the number of disciples in Jerusalem increased greatly; even great numbers of men and women became believers. Thus, many of the people in the area carried the sick out into the streets and laid them on mats so that when Peter came by, they could be cured.

During this time period, there broke out a severe persecution of the church in Jerusalem and the surrounding area. Many followers were scattered to the winds as they fled for safety. Now Saul, who was an elite soldier of the Roman legion, consented to many of the executions. Infact, still breathing murderous threats against the disciples of the Lord, went to the high priest. Once there he asked him for letters to the synagogues in Damascus to allow him to arrest any men or women who belonged to the Way. He wanted to bring them back to Jerusalem in chains to discredit and humiliate them.

There have been many such perilous periods in history where our world is lost in morals and no thought about the kingdom of God. This was the case as Saul journeyed to Damascus. While on his journey, a light from the sky suddenly flashed around him. He fell to the ground and heard a voice saying to him, "Saul, Saul, why are you persecuting me?"

Upon being blinded, Saul asked who was addressing him and had a reply from the Lord that indeed, he is Jesus. And he gave Saul instructions on where to proceed and what to do. The men who were traveling with him stood speechless, for they heard the voice but could not see anyone. Since Saul was struck blind, he had to be led by the hand as they proceeded to Damascus. For three days he was unable to see, eat or drink!

In the interim, there was a disciple in Damascus named Ananias who the Lord spoke to in a vision. The Lord instructed Ananias to go to the house of Judas, and ask for a man by the name of Saul from Tarsus. To both men the Lord gave visions of instructions on what was to take place.

Ananias proceeded to find Saul and obeyed the instructions of the Lord by laying his hands on him and thus he gained back his eyesight. For Saul was a chosen instrument to carry the Lord's name before the Gentiles, kings and the Israelites. Once Saul got up after regaining his eyesight, he was baptized and received the Holy Spirit. Hence, he became a bulwark of the faith for teaching the Word of God and composing many letters of instruction.

At this time many of the apostles feared Saul and rightly so, due to his relentless persecutions. God in his wisdom sent a vision to Peter three times to reinforce the message that, "What God has made clean, you are not to call profane." From that point on Saul, a soldier and persecutor of Christians, became known as Paul, missionary crusader for the church of Christianity.

One could say that a paradigm shift took place in the practice of the faith, not with the blood of goats and calves any more, but with the blood of Jesus, thus obtaining eternal redemption. Each of us now must eat the Lord's body and drink his blood to enter the heavenly Kingdom of God.

The apostles along with Paul set out to all points of the compass to carry on Jesus's mission to teach, heal and proclaim God's word to all who would hear in the sacrificial elements of life, bread and wine. They become the Body and Blood of Christ and the only thing each person has to do is draw near with faith, eat and drink.

By word of mouth, they proceeded for there were no radios, TV's or internet. No jet planes or trains but only by foot or beast to travel. If they traveled by sea then by ship they went and it took months, not days to reach their destination. The desire to spread the faith burned within their hearts and a devotion of duty to God within their souls. Hardships, persecutions, and calumny was their rewards.

The whole world eventually learned what happened to Judas, who hung himself in despair, no more needs to be said. Andrew the brother of Simon Peter became a missionary to modern day Georgia and Bulgaria. He eventually was martyred, crucified in the town of Achaia, the smallest country in the Peloponnesus of what is now present-day Greece.

Bartholomew who was originally from Cana in Galilee and known as Nathanael, preached in Turkey and moved south-east to Iraq, Iran, Afghanistan, Pakistan and then India. There was no limit or zeal of the apostles once guided by the Holy Spirit.

Picture from Creative Commons

He was eventually crucified with his head downward and buried in Allanum, a town of Armenia.

Then there was James who was the son of Alphaeus, possibly the brother of Matthew. He stayed in the city of Jerusalem to preach and met his end by being stoned to death and buried there beside the temple.

Now the other James was a local missionary in Judea and the son of Zebedee, brother to John. He was referred to by Jesus as one of the sons of thunder. For his efforts to bring the teachings of Jesus in Judea, he was beheaded by Herod the tetrarch and was buried there.

Matthew, a tax collector in Capernaum, the son of Alphaeus was also known as Levi or the publican who went on to write the Gospel of Matthew. An instrumental missionary to Parthia which is modern day Iran, lived a long life and eventually died of old age.

Then yes, there was Simon Peter, the fisherman whom Jesus called to be fishers of men. Also called Cephas who was the brother to Andrew wrote the 1st and 2nd Peter and was an ambitious sort who travelled untiringly to Pontus, Galatia, Cappadocia, Italy, and Asia. His efforts were extensive and worked with Paul laying the foundation of the Church throughout the area. After their departure, Mark, who was the interpreter for Peter, went on to write his version of the Gospel. Eventually he was crucified by Nero in Rome with his head downward, a request by Peter himself because he didn't feel worthy to be crucified like Jesus. The guilt for denying Jesus resonated throughout his life, hence the feelings of feeling unworthy.

Philip, the disciple who asked Jesus to show us the Father, completely exasperated Jesus! For Jesus replied to Philip that after all the time he was with them, all the disciples should know by now that whoever has seen me has seen the Father! He originally came from Bethsaida and preached in Phrygia or present-day Turkey. He was also crucified in Hierapolis with his head downward during the time of the ruler, Domitian.

A Believer

Then there was Simon who was from Cana, the place where Jesus performed one of his first miracles at the wedding of Cana. Better known as Simon the Canaanite or Simon the Zealot and son of Clopas. The Zealots were Jewish revolutionaries who opposed Rome. He became the second bishop of Jerusalem and was one of the few that lived to the ripe old age of 120 years.

Jude, son of James also had the name of Thaddaeus which meant warm-hearted, preached in Edessa and all of Mesopotamia corresponding to present-day Iraq, Syria, Turkey and Iran. He too had a long life and died of old age.

Many will not forget Thomas, also known as Didymus, often remembered as "Doubting Thomas," preached to the Parthians, Medes, Persians and Hyrcanians. He was speared in four different places with a pine spear at Calamene, a city of India and was buried there.

Matthias, was a local missionary in Jerusalem. After Jesus' ascension, the 11 Apostles met in the upper room where they were staying and cast lots to decide between two disciples, Matthias and Joseph also called Barsabbas, who was surnamed Justus. Matthias was selected to replace the dastardly bastard Judas Iscariot to bring the Apostles number back to the original twelve and was one of the 72 of expanded missionaries. He died there and was buried in Jerusalem.

Paul, the bulwark of Christianity, became an apostle a year after the ascension of Christ and beginning at Jerusalem advanced as far as Illyricum or present-day Croatia, Italy, Spain and throughout the region preaching the Gospel for 35 years. During the time of Nero, he was beheaded and buried in Rome.

Last but certainly not least, John, the son of Zebedee and brother to James and identified as the disciple "whom Jesus loved", wrote the Gospel of John. He also wrote 1st, 2nd and 3rd John and was eventually banished by King Domitian to the isle of Patmos where he wrote the Book of Revelation about the upcoming apocalypse. John was one of the few disciples that did not die a cruel death, although he was a prisoner for years, but died of old age in Ephesus.

The magnanimous beginnings of the Holy Church through the Messiah, Jesus Christ, the only begotten Son of God and through the efficacy of the works of the Holy Spirit who guided the original 14 disciples to spread the Good News; the church still flourishes two thousand years later. Out of 14 disciples, the beginning twelve, plus Matthias to replace Judas, and Paul, the bulwark of Christian teachings, one was lost forever and nine were martyred.

A Believer

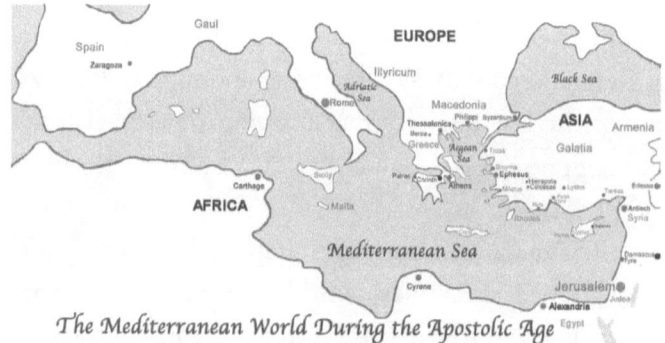

The Mediterranean World During the Apostolic Age

Picture from Creative Commons

Chapter 3

Anatolia or Bust

Asia Minor is the most western region of Asia and is the largest section of modern-day Turkey. Asia Minor is also called Anatolia. In the second millennium B.C. this nation was the center of the Hittite Empire. Following the Dorian invasion, Greeks migrated to Asia Minor and in 546 B.C. the Persian King Cyrus II conquered the land. This was followed by the conquest by Alexander the Great. Destiny moves on for fame, fortune or doom while most of Asia Minor becomes part of the Roman and Byzantine Empires. This is a land that knows conquest; this is the land evangelized by both St. Paul and St. John with a different conquest of the spirit. Now destiny moves on for God, versus glory or gold.

The miracle of Pentecost was the crowning point, the piece de resistance for the disciples which armed them with the knowledge, courage, wisdom and fortitude to persevere throughout the world spreading the Good News. The souls of the apostles were ready! The apostle John, the youngest of all apostles and the one that Jesus loved, bolstered with fortitude by the Holy Spirit and the wisdom of the divinity of the Messiah proceeded to Anatolia to do his part of spreading the Good News after establishing his evangelical mission in Jerusalem with Peter. Peter, who was commissioned as head of the new church by Christ, whom the keys of heaven were given, paired with John as they become the dynamic duo, one the apostle of love, the other the apostle of inspired divinity.

But first they needed to heed the words of their messiah, the Shepherd of the flock, who commanded them to first, tend to my sheep. And who were the sheep, but the obstinate Jews of Israel? How many of us have ears to hear but do not heed the words of our loving Savior?

The first-fruits of the Good News began in that ancient abode of Jerusalem which was met with much resistance like a firewall! The Herodians who ruled, profaned anything religious and preferred orgies, the Pharisees who exercised fallacious worship and did not understand the sacredness of God and finally the Sadducees, who did not believe in the resurrection and the precious gift of redemption, eternal life! This indeed was the firewall that overshadowed the Gift to pass on to the Gentiles. Thanks be to God!

Peter who stood up before the cohorts of the time, addressed them and I am definitely paraphrasing here to drive home a point, accursed them by saying, you blasphemous idiots, you damnable fools who condemned and crucified our Lord!

No wonder, the gift of redemption was opened up for all who believe and now you know the rest of the story of the gentiles. Thanks be to God; we have a chance!

The apostles were at the Temple and the first Christian manifestation was an act of sheer kindness, a miracle of benevolence. At the entrance of the Temple was a street person, a beggar who was an invalid from birth. He needed aid and sought to seek it from Peter and John who were about to enter the Temple. Asking for alms, the beggar requested either gold or silver; Peter told the beggar that he had neither. But he continued by saying, "what I do have, I give to you and told him to get up and walk." The beggar arose and immediately walked and rejoiced.

That one beggar symbolizes the cripples of our world, not so much in physical ailments but the disabled individuals with fractured hearts, ruptured souls and unwholesome minds who do not do the will of God. That transitional period was difficult for the apostles, the people and furthermore, God our heavenly Father. That period from the passion, crucifixion, resurrection and the ascension is a dichotomous period between good and evil. The necessity of Christ's death for redemption and the inception of the Holy Spirit to inaugurate the Holy Church was good for humanity. But it was also the colophon of satan who presumptuously thought he had won a victory by instigating the betrayal of Jesus through Judas. The first colophon of satan was instigating the fall of the angels in heaven, the second, the temptation of Adam and Eve in the garden the third failed attempt is the temptation of Christ in the desert and now the crucifixion of our Lord.

Peter clearly believed in Jesus and John clearly loved our Lord, and it is in that name that believers will walk in heaven! The corteges of dissidents, the Sadducees, Pharisees, Kings and public officials along with the existing chief-priest accused and blasphemed our Lord and when Peter stood-up to admonish them and the Israelites with these words, and again I am paraphrasing, you Israelites who think that you know the Torah and understood that God sent the Patriarchs, Abraham, Isaac, Jacob and Joseph; He who has glorified Jesus, His only begotten Son whom you denied and crucified, you belligerent bastards, you denied the Holy and Righteous One and released a murderer. Peter was eloquent and did not mince any of his words as he continued, the author of life you put to death, but God raised him from the dead; of this we are witnesses. A conundrum for many but not for believers.

As they continued speaking to the people, a cohort of priests, the captain of the temple guard, and the Sadducees confronted and arrested them. Eventually both Peter and John were released because everyone living in Jerusalem knew about the remarkable sign of the beggar at the temple and the deniability wasn't at all possible by them. During the high-priesthood of Annas and Caiaphas of the Sanhedrin, their belligerent, haughty disposition was contrary to the will of God. Instead of upholding the very name of God; they blasphemed his name, and there is no other name under the heavens whereby all of humanity may be saved.

Clearly to be a Christian, a follower of Jesus Christ is not for the faint-hearted but for those willing to standup and give witness even unto death. Infact, James, the brother of John was the first of the Apostles who suffered martyrdom. The early Christian Church fell under intense persecution and continual scrutiny by the Roman leaders especially beginning with Nero. But it was through the remarkable witness of Christian martyrdom that led to the continued expansion of the faith.

Satan had his hooks into the family of the Herodians for it was Herod Agrippa who thus shed the blood of the apostle James, the one cradled and grew in the incest and orgies of the palace of Tiberius and inherited the corrupt morals of the worst persecutors. His grandfather, Herod the Great, was indeed the murderer of the infants of Bethlehem who tried to deceive the Magi in telling the location of the infant birth of our Lord. His sister was none other then the adulterous Herodias who had demanded the head of John the Baptist. Whew, the family from hell!

A Believer

During the persecution, the fish became the symbol of the Christian faith, adorning places of meetings and early Christian Churches. In a time when professing your faith was very precarious and an invitation to death, the fish became the secret code of the day. The fish captures the essential creed of our Christian faith, for the Greek word for fish is ιχθυς or ichthus, an acronym and acrostic for **Jesus Christ, Son of God, Savior**. One Christian would draw a curve representing half of the symbol, and another follower would complete the cryptic symbol by drawing the other curve.

The beginnings of the Christian Church were unsurmountable at times especially since intense persecution under Roman rulers lasted nearly 300 years, until the emperor Constantine issued the Edict of Milan in 313 AD which mandated complete toleration of Christianity throughout the Roman Empire.

Jesus Christ, Son of God, Savior

Ι   Χ   Υ   Θ   Σ

Ιησους	ι	Jesus
Χριστος	χ	Christ
Θεου	θ	of God
Υιος	υ	Son
Σωτηρ	ς	Savior

Image from Creative Commons

The martyrdom of the Apostle James, the brother of John, was the signal, the very impetus for the first dispersion of the Apostles to their missionary genesis. The most important conquest for the faith is initiated by the youthful Paul of Tarsus. Never had the apostolate a better recruit than that Pharisee, Jew by origin, Greek by his native land, Roman by his right of citizenship and above all, the inception by Jesus Christ to preach to the Gentiles. Wow, again I say wow! What more can be said of Paul, a bulwark of the faith. He had come to Jerusalem to confer with the first missionaries of the Gospel of Jesus Christ. And the pillars of the Church, the Apostles including John gave him fellowship. That is probably the first time we behold Paul with John and likewise the last.

The Apostle John embarked for Asia and began his sojourn at Ephesus. His beginning journey by ship began at the port of Joppa, one of the oldest cities and working harbors for commerce. It was the chief seaport of ancient Israel, located on a sandy promontory between Caesarea and Gaza, about thirty miles northwest of Jerusalem. Located within the tribal land of Dan, it belonged to the Phoenicians for years. Peter had come to Joppa from Lydda to spread the Good News, evangelize and perform the miracle of raising Tabitha or Dorcas from the dead.

A Believer

Climbing aboard one of the many commercial corn ships John received a salutation of, "Top of the morning," from one of the mates.

John always replied to any greeting with, "The Lord is risen!"

Ships of this size usually had a tonnage around 2,600 tons with a hull that traverse to either a bird's figurehead carving, or some other creature, above the bow and a bird's-tail at the stern. In the midst was a high mast, usually of cedar wood and near the prow was a smaller one for hoisting a small sail. All passengers were asked to go below before leaving port so the crew could rig the sails and prepare to heave-ho. Once the ship was under way, passengers could come topside. From his beginnings as a fisherman, John was accustomed to sailing and enjoyed the brief trip and the brisk air. It helped to clear his mind and prepare himself for his forthcoming challenges at Ephesus.

Ephesus, the jewel of Asia Minor, founded primarily by those from the ancient Greek city of Athens. She was the capital of Ionia and was originally called Arsinoe after the second wife of one of its governors. The closest of Revelation's seven churches to the island of Patmos where the apostle John wrote his book of Revelation. An advantageous location of the city made it the chief city of Asia Minor for it maintained an artificial harbor accessible to the largest ships of the time. Ephesus stood at the entrance of a valley that reached far into the spreading province. The ease of traveling to her, by either land or sea, made it the most accessible populated destination in Asia. Five hundred cities strewn along the majestic shore-line of Anatolia and amongst them, Ephesus was the queen.

The city possesses a plethora of the most eminent orators, speakers, con-artist and shysters in the world. Everything was preached there! From monotheism of One God by St. Paul and St. John, to polytheism of many gods, Gnosticism, dualism and the list went on and on. Both Paul and John certainly had their missionary missions of spreading the Gospel commissioned for them and it might have been a mission impossible; except for the divinity of Jesus Christ and the inspiration of the Holy Spirit to bolster them to persevere.

And persevere they did, spreading the Word of God, the Good News! The field of credence was prepared and the seed of faith was spread but not all believed. The disciples' efforts were met with a mixture of acceptance, rejoicing and resistance. Beyond their years of discipleship, the apostles taught throughout the known world, delivering the possessed, healing the sick and beckoning the conquests of the faith to the point that the established worship was appalled and alarmed. Their progress was spreading like wild-fire and their efforts were met with resistance, riots, martyrdom and persecution.

A Believer

But during this time the good fight was continued by others, thus St. Paul portrayed to us Timothy, the good soldier of Christ. The efforts and good fight continue and many joined in the effort. Nourished in the Holy Scripture, imposition by many hands; the work of Christ progressed. Oh, how greatly the Apostle John must of loved the young priest, Timothy, whose soul was so perfectly assimilated to his own for they persevered in Ephesus together.

John tirelessly labored and established churches throughout Asia Minor and seven of these early major churches became known as the Seven Churches of the Apocalypse. Infused with the Holy Spirit, John, Peter and Paul along with all of the apostles spread the faith tirelessly. Since the Spirit has been given to humanity as the source of unity between God, soul and church, His Grace continually nurtures us in the body and blood of our Lord, Jesus Christ. Grace is God's free and forgiving self-communication that enables humans to share in that divine love. Jesus Christ became human so that he could die for us and in-turn each of us could share in his divinity.

Humanity's Paradox

Picture from Creative Commons

As the leader of the missionary effort to the Asian churches, John was targeted by Roman authorities and exiled to Patmos Island where he received the apocalyptic visions. From his confinement in prison and the inspiration from the divine visions, he pursued writing his books of the fourth Gospel, his three Letters and last but not least, the Book of Revelation on the final days of humanity. The very times and places aren't very clear but the essence of his writings gives us a transparency of the divinity of Jesus and warnings against false teachings. The letters of John were probably written while in Ephesus for the flock of believers.

These are the spiritual fields that St. John and St. Paul sowed, preached in, prayed and was accustomed to regenerate souls in the breaking of the bread. From the Last Supper where Jesus Christ told all of his apostles that they must partake of his body and blood for this is the new covenant of eternal life. Many others joined the flock and those that upheld the Word of God, paid the price. Stephen who was righteous and helped the widows, orphaned and poor joined the disciples and spoke the truth. His efforts were paid in full as he was hauled from the city by the pretentious Jews and stoned to death.

Throughout the years and hence centuries, many more have joined the flock and God's Word remains everlasting. From the inception of the apostles, the neophytes of the new faith to the Christendom of St. Paul by Jesus Christ, the only begotten Son of God, and through the works of the Holy Spirit, the mustard seed of faith was nourished, grew and spread to encompass the world. And when the faithful flocked to John, he did not hand them the cup which inebriated the disciples of Socrates in the symposia, but gave them to drink of the chalice which he was given from the hand of Jesus at the Last Supper. The world grew from the ashes of the seditious rebellions of Satan, first in heaven and then on earth; God is always in control and sent His only begotten Son as a propitiation for us to follow Him as the Way, the Truth and the Life.

Ephesus was the recipient of two great saints, John and Paul, who believed in Holiness from above. That this life of holiness was the life of God himself as the testament of St. John says, "My little children, to be of God and in God, is to walk even as he walked."

And the words of St. Paul to the Ephesians, "Be imitators of God, as his dear children."

Meanwhile, the blueprint of worship was laid down, together with the morality in the church of Ephesus.

The birth of Christianity had its labor pains for arose the dualism of Gnosticism; one proceeded from the Jews and reformed the Mosaic Law; the other arose from the Gentiles, transforming their religion and philosophy many times over. Many false prophets arose and their speech spread life wildfire, a cancer that could not be contained. Split into sects which breed many more sects and the chain reaction never stops like nuclear fission waiting for the fusion. That fusion will be the second coming of Christ our Lord!

Thus, from the very beginnings of the early church in Ephesus, the evil one masturbated his seeds to seize control of the sects for possession of mankind. Satan did this through a threefold process of pride through rationalism, the flesh through sensualism, hence the abominations of the LGBTQ, which Paul made

A Believer

transparent with dotting the "i's" and crossing the "t's" in his first epistle to the Romans, and finally the heart through mysticism. The perverted are allowed to wallow in their perversions. Such is the stage of life. May God have mercy on their souls!

Never forget the words that come from the Book of Wisdom which says,

> "God did not make death,
> nor does he rejoice in the destruction of the living.
> For he fashioned all things that they might have being;
> and the creatures of the world are wholesome,
> and there is not a destructive drug among them
> nor any domain of the netherworld on earth,
> for justice is undying.
> For God formed man to be imperishable;
> the image of his own nature he made him.
> But by the envy of the devil, death entered the world,
> and they who belong to his company experience it.
> But the souls of the just are in the hands of God,
> and no torment shall touch them."

Now by the grace of God, and by the propitiation of His only Son, our Lord, we have the divine mercy of redemption which the fallen angels and Satan do not have. Think about that! For once the trumpets are blown and Jesus Christ returns in His Glory; we will be rewarded for our choices in this life to either Heaven or Hell!

The inception for the apostle John in Anatolia was far from welcoming! Like a whirlwind of hail, thunder and lightning, John, Paul and all the other missionary disciples were inundated with attacks from all fronts. These threats were coercions which came like punches to dissolve the faith in three major waves. One could not duck or avoid them, but meet them head-on to protect the new faith of Christ and deter the onslaught.

The newly appointed Bishop's of the church were concerned and appealed to the Apostle John to write a Gospel to explain the divinity of Christ to combat the three main pillories of the faith. The first was the denial of Christ's Divinity which led to many heresies. The second denial was of Christ's two natures and the third denial was of Christ's humanity which gave rise to Docetism and many forms of Gnosticism. From the entire group of the apostles, Peter, James and John were among the earliest of Jesus' disciples who had been with Him the longest. (Lk 5:4-11). These three disciples were present with Jesus during divine spiritual events and eyewitnesses of Jesus raising Jairus's daughter from the dead (Lk 8:49-56), witness the transfiguration of Jesus along with Moses and Elijah (Mk 9:2-3), and accompanying Him while Jesus devotedly prayed in the Garden of Gethsemane (Mt 26:36-38). Three witnesses to three monumental events revealing the glory and darkest trials of Christ our Lord.

John was also there at the foot of the Cross with the blessed Mother of Jesus through his agony, sufferings and pain where Jesus looked at His Mother and the apostle that He loved and said, "Behold your son … behold your mother (Jn 19:26-27).

All of these impressions left an indelible memory of the person who is and always will be the Son of God, both human and divine sent to save the world!

John had the supreme task to record the divinity of Christ and since he was there, remembered them well to illuminate His Divinity and the words that Jesus spoke,

> I am the bread of life. (Jn 6:35, 48, 51)
> I am the light of the world. (Jn 8:12, 9:5)
> I am the gate of the sheep. (Jn 10:7, 9)
> I am the good shepherd. (Jn 10:11, 14)
> I am the resurrection and the life. (Jn 11:25)
> I am the way, the truth and the life. (Jn 14:6
> I am the true vine. (Jn 15:1)

These seven "I am," statements are revelations of who Jesus is and further proof is given by the miracles that he performed. These are written that you may believe that Jesus is the Christ, the Son of the God and by believing, you may have eternal life. (Jn 20:30-31).

John followed the very steps of Jesus and from His Baptism to the Last Supper, to the Agony in the Garden, His arrest, sufferings, crucifixion and resurrection was illumined to see the divinity of Christ. And from the Ascension and Descent of the Holy Spirit, John's soul was enkindled to envision the heavenly kingdom. The vision of the eye to see is limited, but an enkindled soul by the Holy spirit gives vision which is limitless! True profundity of intelligence of the divine can only come from God. God's ultimate word is Jesus Christ!

The influence of Jesus Christ on the apostle John led his very steps to Anatolia and the Church spread throughout Asia Minor as well as other parts of the world. Through the divine intervention of one person's birth, the One who dies for all, transforms the world through twelve apostles and the Holy Spirit. Think about that! From His propitiation for all of our sins, to the proliferation of the church, God's Word and Will is revealed, elucidated, and illumined throughout the earth.

As the Church grew and spread like wild fire, the local and ruling authorities were intimidated that their control over their subjects would dissolve. John became the cynosure of their rage for his evangelizing, anointing bishops and spreading the truth about Jesus and against sin. For the light of the world and our truth is Jesus, the Son of God. Against everything that is good, pure and holy is the master of hell, who wants to reap the sinners of this world. Jesus came to save us sinners and the devil wants to condemn all sinners to his realm of eternal fire.

This tug of souls has been an enigma for humanity since the beginning of creation. For the last two thousand years, the Gospel has unceasingly given Hope to the world and an opportunity for salvation to those who repent and seek forgiveness through the Divine Mercy of Christ. Each of us in-turn must take-up the Gospel, our lectio divina, divine reading to reflect, pray and imbibe the truth.

It was the emperor Domitian who learned that the disciple that Jesus loved was still living in Ephesus spreading the Good News. And this emperor Domitian who sought his subjects' worship and whose father, Vespasian, levied a temple tax on the Jews, extended the tax to all Christians. Now in his complete avariciousness, wanted it all! His subjects to pay the tax and worship his very being. And from a letter addressed by his proconsul in Ephesus, to the supreme Caesar Domitian which told of the marvelous deeds of St. John, enraged him to the ends of the earth.

John was arrested, shackled with the weight of chains and hauled to the Porta Latina, the Latin Gate which was a single arch in the Aurelian Walls of Rome. There was no justice in those days, just the whims and vicissitudes of the emperor as the wind blows and no recourse but accept the verdict. For John the verdict was straightforward; death during the eras of the Caesars always included sinister torture for the ruling authorities savored the moments to watch their victims in torment. John was to be boiled in oil for the screams were to be heard beyond the walls of Rome.

The cauldron was filled, the fire beneath was lit and the victim was led to his demise. John was the last of the apostles and suffered the loss of his Messiah to crucifixion, along with the loss of his brother, James to martyrdom. Peter along with many of the other disciples, including the bulwark Paul were already martyred. The sorrow and deep grief at times was too much to bear for John.

Hauled from his cell, the shackles untethered and dumped into the cauldron should have been the end to John. But as fate proceeds from God, divine intervention extinguished the fire below and it could not be relit. Foiled again Caesar? Due to the embarrassment and inconvenience of Caesar's guess who thrilled at the delight of watching, John was banished to the outer regions of the empire, Patmos.

What can be said about Patmos a small Greek Island in the Aegean Sea? The most desolate of islands in the archipelago, a rocky, barren island where many criminals of Rome were sent to work in the mines for the rest of their lives. But this would not be the end of John! This man who was inspired for three years to follow the footsteps of the Messiah, witness the divinity of His miracles, passion and death was about to receive the greatest visions of all; the end of the world.

John had finished his Gospel on the divinity of Christ, the three epistles about the attributes of morality for God, truth, Christology and mutual love. Now he would write the most compelling book about the futuristic visions of the Second Coming and the end

A Believer

of the world. For he wrote the very last book of the Bible. The most difficult to understand for it is full of extravagant symbolism and beyond our comprehension. One needs to read the book slowly and then pray, reflect and contemplate it's meaning. Pray for the wisdom from God to understand, reflect the ultimate purpose of its themes and then reread and contemplate the purpose for each of the remaining souls. For this is the destiny for all! It reveals the how's, when's, where's, what's and even the why's. Why?

Why you may ask? Because life is a precious gift and yet God loved us enough to give us freedom of choice. We can choose to believe, trust and follow his commandments for God so loved the world that He sent His only begotten Son, that whoever should believe in Him might have eternal life. But many in the world back then and many more today, choose to follow the one who has fallen from heaven and through his pride causes us to transgress from God. That is why! And only God knows the appointed time for the Second Coming. Christ came the first time in divine mercy. The second time will be for our final Judgement. Hopefully the reader will have a feeling of horror for apostasy and rebellion that will be severely punished by God.

This is the revelation of Jesus Christ, which God through an angel envisioned to John, the last of the Apostles, and the message was clear. He was instructed to write and preserve what he will see and hear.

There are two essential natures that one must understand to comprehend the Book of Revelation. And it is simply this; the beginning of the book reveals to us one major truth, "I am the Alpha and the Omega," says the Lord God, "the one who is and who was and who is to come, the Almighty."

> "Behold, he is coming amid the clouds,
> and every eye will see him,
> even those who pieced him.
> All the peoples of the earth will lament him."
> Yes, Amen.

The second nature is from the second letter of Peter 3:3-10.

"Know this first of all, that in the last days scoffers will come to scoff, living according to their own desires and saying, 'where is the promise of his coming? From the time when our ancestors fell asleep, everything has remained as it was from the beginning of creation.' They deliberately ignore the fact that the heavens existed of old and earth was formed out of water and through water by the word of God; through these the world that then existed was destroyed, deluged with water. The present heavens and earth have been reserved by the same word for fire, kept for the day of judgment and of destruction of the godless."

A Believer

"But do not ignore this one fact, beloved, that with the Lord one day is like a thousand years and a thousand years like one day. The Lord does not delay his promise, as some regard "**delay**," but he is patient with you, not wishing that any should perish but that all should come to repentance. But the day of the Lord will come like a thief, and then the heavens will pass away with a mighty roar and the elements will be dissolved by fire, and the earth and everything done on it will be found out."

The Book of Revelation has its origin in a time of crisis, but it remains valid and meaningful for Christians of all time and especially for now! Today all Christians face insuperable evil and all Christians are called to trust in the Words of Jesus, "Behold, I am with you always, until the end of the age." Mt 28;20.

Now due to the multiple numerologies, incomprehensible symbolisms and unlimited, allegorical rhubarbs of descriptions, an average person like myself is lost. God in His divine wisdom only reveals truths to the pure of heart, and Jesus in His divine mercy only speaks to us in parables. If, and this is a big "If," we truly ask in prayer, seek in sincerity and patiently knock continuously, then and only then will answers be revealed.

The vision came to John as a prisoner on the island of Patmos to address all of the apparitions to the beginning seven churches in Asia Minor of the known world. And hence, in-turn to all the churches of the world today! We begin with the trumpet blast to awaken the world that His time has come. Just like when the Great Theophany on the morning of the third day there were peals of thunder and lightning with a heavy cloud over Mount Sinai when Moses came to God.

In Revelation we now learn of the seven stars and seven lampstands along with a sharp two-edged sword coming out of the mouth of the Son of Man and His face shone like the sun at its brightness. The seven stars are the angels of the seven churches and the seven lampstands are the seven churches in the beginning of Christianity.

The vision addresses a distinct message for each of the seven churches and then a vision of an open door to heaven to reveal heavenly worship of God and the Lamb. John was lifted in spirit to witness the heavenly throne and around the throne of God four creatures that symbolized respectively what is noblest, strongest, wisest and swiftest in creation. The four living creatures, each with six wings kept exclaiming,

> "Holy, holy, holy is the Lord God Almighty,
> who was, and who is, and who is to come."

Then John saw a scroll in the right hand of the one who sat on the throne. It had writing on both sides and was sealed with seven seals. Then John saw a mighty angel who proclaimed in a loud voice, "Who is worthy to open the scroll and break its seals?" The scroll is God's plan for the world and only the Lamb has the right to carry

A Believer

out the divine plan. Christ is the Paschal Lamb without blemish whose blood saved us through his divine mercy. A series of seven disasters begins as each seal is broken. The seventh seal is opened and heralds the beginning of the sounding of the Seven Trumpets to initiate the Great Tribulation. The first six sounds of the trumpets result in various plagues and chastisements on the wicked. The crescendo builds till the seventh trumpet announces the Second Coming of Jesus and the Rapture. Then comes the two End-time prophets who will be the vanguard of God's witnesses in the Tribulation.

John is told about the beast and the False Prophet and the Battle of the great day of the Lord, commonly known as Armageddon. Then a great sign appeared in the sky, a woman clothed with the sun, with the moon under her feet, and on her head a crown of twelve stars. She was with child and wailed aloud in pain as she labored to give birth. Then another sign appeared in the sky; it was a huge red dragon. This portrays the power of evil, represented by the dragon, in opposition to God, first in heaven then on earth against humanity and against the birth of His only begotten Son, then the Son and finally the church of believers; the spiritual tug of war for souls to enter either heaven or hell. For what is revealed to John is the spiritual kaleidoscope of life; Heaven, the downfall of the angels, creation and temptation of humanity, the Son of God, and the Holy Church.

For John proclaims that he saw a beast with ten horns and seven heads; on its horns were ten diadems, and on the heads blasphemous names. Only through divine wisdom could one comprehend and begin to understand this divine revelation. For the revelation continuous to cover the imprisonment of Satan, the magnanimous 1,000-year reign of Jesus and His saints on Earth, battle of Gog and Magog which occurs at the end of the Millennium when Satan reappears for a short season, and the final destruction of the surface of the earth as we now know it. The vision continues with the Great White Throne Judgment and the glorious Heavenly City that descends for the blessed future that awaits all believers. These visions of Revelation give us the warnings, predictions and the final perspectives of the celestial commitments from God. At some point in our present time there will be a crossroads of convergence of ideologies, leadership and conditions that will erupt like a volcano and God's Judgement will prevail.

The best advise for believers is simply this, follow not the bad or evil, but that which is good. And this is exactly what John did his entire life for whoever does good, is of God; whoever does evil, does not know God.

Patmos Island and the vision was not the end for the last apostle, for John was released from prison after the death of the tyrant that put him there in the first place. John returned to Ephesus and founded more churches, established more bishops and continued the service of

A Believer

God. God fearing men who were designated to him by the sign of the Holy Spirit to continue the work of Jesus to save souls. And these names remain in history such as Ignatius and Polycarp and who were instrumental to continue the work of Jesus Christ. Along with these souls is one remarkable witness who gives testimony of the faith in Jesus Christ before the emperor of Rome at the Pergamum gladiator games. His name is Antipas and followed the example of Christ by giving his life for another.

Chapter 4

Who is this Antipas?

Any edifice needs a strong foundation to stand firm, a ship a sturdy keel to withstand the mighty seas, and a church a cornerstone to build upon. Jesus Christ is that cornerstone of the Holy Church and the apostles are the pillars of the faith from which the multitude of the faithful grow. And for the faithful to grow, flourish and understand the teachings of the faith, there has to be a bulwark to teach the faith. St. Paul was that bulwark to explain the principles of Christianity in his epistles to many of the churches. The protector of the faith and church is the Holy Spirit. Each individual is called through Baptism to remain diligent in the faith and that diligence is between you and God, and the final say on that will be Jesus Christ at the Judgement.

Our Messiah, Jesus, told us that he is the way, the truth and the life. St. Paul was instrumental to teach and convey those very sentiments in his many letters as he says to the Ephesians,

"Blessed be the God and Father of our Lord Jesus Christ, who has blessed us in Christ with every spiritual blessing in the heavens, as he chose us in him, before the foundation of the world, to be holy and without blemish before him.

In love he destined us for adoption to himself through Jesus Christ, in accord with the favor of his will, for the praise of the glory of his grace that he granted us in the beloved.

In him we have redemption by his blood, the forgiveness of transgressions, in accord with the riches of his grace that he lavished upon us.

In all wisdom and insight, he has made known to us the mystery of his will in accord with his favor that he set forth in him as a plan for the fullness of times, to sum up all things in Christ, in heaven and on earth.

In him we were also chosen, destined in accord with the purpose of the One who accomplishes all things according to the intention of his will, so that we might exist for the praise of his glory, we who first hoped in Christ.

In him you also, who have heard the word of truth, the gospel of your salvation, and have believed in him, were sealed with the promised Holy Spirit, which is the first installment of our inheritance toward redemption as God's possession, to the praise of his glory." Eph 1:3-14.

Humanity's Paradox

This city Pergamum where art thou? In Anatolia, today's Turkey, from the city of Ephesus to Smyrna was a four-day walk due north. And from that city another four to five-day walk northward to Pergamum. The hearty and strong could make the overall journey in six-days. The average person in eight-days, but the weaken person rested in Smyrna and tally-ho on in nine days. The nobles and wealthy rode either a horse or stagecoach and turned up their noses as they passed by the pedestrian peasants.

Like the gods on Mt. Olympus, Pergamum was a city of significant stature with much beautification of libraries, coliseum's, temples and statues to impress the multitude of affluence, commercialism and wealth. But Almighty God is not impressed with adornment of the frivolous of society. And if humanity does not understand that, then we are lost to our devious, self-centered selves and the woes of satan!

One needs to ask so what is the zeitgeist of that era? It was a time when the elite were opulent, the emperors and ruling class were barbaric and the majority of people ignorant of God. Does this sound familiar? Throughout the millenniums of history, the process becomes decadent and collapses within their own fallacious ways.

And whom was this person known as Antipas who resided in the city of Pergamum that we see mentioned in the book of revelation by John the Apostle? Why is he so important to mention above all other names? First, we

A Believer

must look at the city and from that decadence see why Antipas becomes loftier then all the other citizens.

There was one individual with a long name such as Lucius Cuspius Pactumeius Rufinus, whom I shall refer to from now on as Ruf! Ruf was a nobleman of Pergamum and under the appointment by the great emperor Domitian had the honor to sponsor two days of gladiatorial contests the following year. The first being in the great month of April and the second before the autumn equinox in September. Beastly, blood thirsty, sordid games to the N-th degree. Gladiatorial bouts, executions, tortures, slaughtered animals and voyeurisms of all sorts. My God; they even had a naked women chained to a bull and both were slaughtered, how gauche?

Now this Antipas, who is the son of a nobleman, and benefactor of two wealthy cities of Tyre and Caesarea is a freeborn citizen of said blessed empire of Rome. He is recruited by Ruf for the multiple tasks of organizing all the affairs of the gladiatorial bouts. From raising funds, invitations, setting-up accommodations and solicitation of gladiators not only from Pergamum, but also from distant cities and even as far away as Egyptian Alexandria. These games were major entertainment for the emperor himself and the senate, to the establish elite of the Roman Empire and precipitated down to the peasants of the empire if they could attend.

Initially, he has objections to the prescheduled games of slaughter and mayhem but does not want to offend the emperor and lose status with his business ventures. There are those who denounce the gladiatorial contest as barbaric that brings shame of infamy to Rome. Ruf reminds Antipas that those that spread critical views of the games need to understand that this is a proficient scheme for the empire to exterminate the dregs of society such as robbers, murderers, treasonous villains, escaped slaves and many foreign prisoners of war. They are the very scourge and underbelly of society.

Ruf continues by telling Antipas that the gladiators exemplify the greatness of Rome by their display of bravery, perseverance and might. Especially the wild-beast hunts which parade a number of exotic animals from all of the known continents. This in-turn exemplified the virtuous and orderly empire versus the savagery, lawlessness of barbarians in the world back then. The problem being who were the barbarians in their life style; the elite, risqué nobility or the roughneck tribes from Germany?

Pergamum, of all the cities of Asia Minor, was by far the most distinguished and had no rivals there. Its impressive location was matched with the most spectacular sacred and royal buildings. The many gods showed favor to Pergamum, including the god of the divine emperor Domitian, which clearly showed that they were the acidic barbarians. With that said, enlightenment only comes from the true God, our heavenly Father through his divine Son Jesus Christ.

A Believer

There was another nobleman of Ephesus who was the son of Theophilus whom had a phenomenal library of manuscripts and scribes to make any copies necessary. Theophilus was part of the elite nobility and basically had no wants. When he died all of his estate was passed on to his son, Calpurnius, including all his servants and scribes. In those days there were no printing presses and if one wanted a copy of a manuscript, then a scribe had to put quill to parchment. The tedious task could take months and even years depending on the size of the manuscript and the diligence of the scribe. No wonder many of the inhabitants throughout the land could not read, let alone write.

The circles of the educated nobility included many people from different paths of life. Not all were haughty, self-indulgent and cynical, infact, there was a young man who was just the opposite and his name is Luke. Luke was well educated, a practicing physician and a good friend to Calpurnius. He had an open mind and heart and cared for people, hence reason enough for him to become a physician to help the infirm. Along comes Paul and befriends Luke teaching him the ways of Christ.

Luke is a phenomenal person and an interesting writer because he did not know Jesus Christ personally. He became a follower of the Lord after his death as Paul tutored him about the Good News. Who better could teach our new disciple about Christ then the man that was blinded by him to follow his ways? A Gentile by birth, he was not one of the original 12 Apostles called by Christ but became one of the 72 disciples accompanying Paul on his missionary journeys after resigning his position as a physician.

One of the most amazing stories Luke wrote about in his Gospel is the birth of the Savior and the Holy Family. And Luke probably got his information about Jesus's birth from none other then Mary herself; who else would have known the particular details of the annunciation by the angel Gabriel, visitation to Elizabeth, the mother of John the Baptist, the visits of the shepherds and the presentation in the Temple. These personal experiences were only known to the mother of our Lord.

The Gospel of Matthew was written basically for the Jews because Matthew was himself a Jew. Mark was written for the Romans and reveals that his Gospel was for a non-Jewish audience. Mark who was an interpreter for Peter simply recorded what Peter preached in Rome. Now comes along Luke who will write the events of Christ for the Gentiles.

One of the major problems, at the time of the birth of our Lord, is even the Jews had sunk into a state of degeneracy in worship to God. The reflecting subjects of the Roman Empire were flagrantly influenced from the multitude of its divinities and offensive features of heathenism. The Gods of antiquity especially those of Greece were of an infamous character. Jupiter, the king of the gods, was deceitful and licentious. Juno, the queen of heaven, was cruel and tyrannical. The Roman gods, Zeus and Themis were no better. What could be expected from those who honored such deities? Even some of the wiser heathens, such as Plato long before the birth of Christ, condemned their mythology as immoral, because all of their transgressions could decay the morals of the Gentiles if they followed suit in their own heavenly worship of One God in three divine persons.

Now this Calpurnius who had a good acquaintance with both Antipas and Luke saw a connecting link between their passions of reading the masterpieces of literature and writing literature that expounds the Word of God. Throughout history very few people could grasp the ideals of life such as Socrates who long before the birth of Messiah said, "Life without truth is not worth living." One can only speculate what his thoughts would be if he could have heard the words of Jesus saying, "I am the way, the truth and the life."

Great minds need to be connected and Calpurnius was the bridge between Antipas and Luke. As if moirai, destinies, has touched their lives Calpurnius explains to Antipas about a close associate whom his father before his death commissioned to write an account about this phenomenal person from Galilee who claims to be the Son of God. He was to include the followers that he chose to start a spiritual awakening. Amongst all nations but especially the Jews, there is a spiritual malaise in worshiping the One God, which is disconcerting.

Antipas upon leaving Caesarea, relocated to Pergamum and engaged in the social and commercial life of both Ephesus and Pergamum. His wealth of exorbitant means allowed him to become a generous philanthropist by multiple contributions for the construction of imperial baths, gymnasiums and libraries along with statuaries of Jupiter, Zeus and their emperor, Domitian. His claim to fame was to make Pergamum a great citadel of the gods.

A fortuitous meeting for Antipas is the friendship that is about to take place; first in his mind, then in his heart and finally in that precious gift of his soul. Luke is no ordinary person and when he puts quill to parchment his words come alive in truth, perception and love. Luke perceives that the quintessence of life is belief in God and that the quietus of life is the final judgment and not death. For death is a door that all of us will pass through for the final judgment. Luke accordingly shifts the early Christian emphasis away from the expectation of an imminent Parousia to the day-to-day concerns of the Christian community in the world, since only God knows the appointed time of the end.

The prologue of the Gospel of Luke clearly shows the reason for its writing as it states, "Since many have undertaken to compile a narrative of the events that have been fulfilled among us, just as those who were eyewitnesses from the beginning and ministers of the word have handed them down to us, I too have decided, after investigating everything accurately anew, to write it down in an orderly sequence for you, most excellent Theophilus, so that you may realize the certainty of the teachings you have received."

Luke understood the meaning of the spiritual fabric of life and wanted to present these themes in his Gospel to teach the Gentiles. From Mary, Luke learns about the circumcision of Jesus and the presentation in the Temple to the Lord, just as it is written in the law of the Lord.

Now there was a man in Jerusalem called Simeon, who was righteous and devout. He was waiting for the consolation of Israel, and the Holy Spirit was on him. Lk 2:25

He was an expert in God's Word, having memorized the first five books of the Bible. Simeon knew the prophecies about the Messiah who was to come and rescue Israel.

There was also a prophetess, Anna, the daughter of Penuel, of the tribe of Asher. She was very old; she had lived with her husband seven years after their marriage, and then was a widow until she was eighty-four. She never left the temple but worshiped night and day, fasting and praying. Coming up to them at that very moment, she gave thanks to God and spoke about the child to all who were looking forward to the redemption of Jerusalem. Lk 2:36-38

These two people exemplified the very essence of the spiritual fabric of life. All believers in Almighty God through Jesus Christ our Lord should make these a daily habit:

- ❖ Prayer
- ❖ Worship
- ❖ Devotion
- ❖ Bible Reading
- ❖ Almsgiving – Our Time, Talent and Treasure

Luke's refreshing Gospel recounts the Life of this Jesus from Nazareth in a new perspective from his nativity to the crucifixion under Pontius Pilate, the governor of Judea. Luke decides to entrust his manuscript to Antipas and explains to him that many of us who call ourselves Christians, do believe this Jesus to be the long-awaited Messiah; the Christ and human incarnation of the most-high God.

Antipas, once he receives the manuscript, cautiously writes to Luke with a strong warning about being careful to associate with these Christians for they are known as the miscreants of society against the emperor. This indeed causes some ambivalence for Luke who thoroughly believes in Jesus as the Messiah. But the present times are very precarious for Christians to meet, socialize and worship together.

In the beginning there weren't many established churches to meet at or formal liturgies to attend. The faithful gathered at a neighbor's home or hall where

A Believer

the anonymous sign of an upper curve was placed over a door's mantle as a foretelling sign of an upcoming meeting. Then the day of the meeting the bottom curve would appear symbolizing a fish and telling all Christians that there is a meeting tonight.

Not wanting to be a curmudgeon and instigate any ill will towards the Christians, Antipas reminded Luke of the Jewish revolt against Roman sovereignty two and a half decades ago. Due to that revolt the armies of Rome decimated many of the Jewish towns in Judea, commenced the displacement of its people and exercised the appropriation of their land. This led to more revolts and escalated tensions against further taxations by Roman authority.

The illustrious general Vespasian was given the task to squelch the rebellion by Nero himself. Vespasian's son Titus was appointed as second-in-command with four legions to assist in eradication of the rebellion. Together their forces launched a persistent campaign to stamp out the rebellion and punish the population for supporting the rebellion.

Due to such a misfortunate end for many of the Jewish people Antipas warns Luke, that he would hate to see a repeat performance of eradication of the Christians since many of them refuse to worship the emperor. And since many of the Judeans were seized and forced to compete in the gladiatorial games, it would be disturbing to see many of the Christians meet the same demise. But revolutionaries deserve death my friend and scoundrels in the world must learn that opposition to Roman rule is futile.

Luke being disturbed with Antipas' views; also understood why he was so prejudiced by his elite status of his lifestyle. He tries to reason with him and find favor by explaining that Jesus came to enlighten us about God's Word and Will. That it doesn't matter if you are rich or poor, clean or unclean, righteous or sinner, now through Jesus, all have a chance to begin anew. This Jesus came to be our light in this tumultuous world.

Luke then made the suggestion to Antipas to attend some of the gatherings of Christians and learn through sharing in a supper, prayer and readings. Then share in open discussion the Word of God and open your heart to Jesus and the Holy Spirit. There are two confirmed meetings that take place in Pergamum at either the house of Antonius whom you already know, and at the house of Kalandion. Keep observant watch for the sign of the fish and the meetings usually take place at either the eighth or ninth hour of the afternoon. The number eight signifying the eight beatitudes that Jesus taught and the ninth hour signifying the nine days between the Ascension of our Lord and the descent of the Holy Spirit upon the Apostles at Pentecost.

And always remember my good friend, Antipas, that "Blessed are the poor in spirit, for theirs is the kingdom of heaven."

A Believer

I am very interested on your impressions of the devout meetings. "Peace be with you in Christ, my friend."

This is all new for Antipas and as the spiritual journey begins, many do not see beyond the end of their spiritual nose. The days should be occupied by daily prayer and devotion. The weeks with worship and gatherings and as the months go by, Antipas has more questions then answers as he puts quill to parchment and ask many questions of Luke. The first of the successive questions begins with why the gatherings and what is this concept of church versus temple? And more importantly, what is this 'Last Supper?'

Luke in receiving the letter by way of his scribe, smiled to himself and pondered how many Gentiles wondered the same thing but were too intimidated to ask. So, Luke puts his quill to parchment, after some considerable prayer and reflection, to reply to Antipas.

My newfound friend, Antipas, our heavenly Father in heaven sent His only begotten Son to show us the way! And this Jesus Christ is His Son who said where two or three are gathered in my name; there I am amongst them. We gather together to give witness to our God through Jesus Christ who died for us. Many were raised to give worship in the Temple. And the Temple is a building, a place for worship or a dwelling place of God or gods.

The church is the human body which the spirit of God dwells in and not just that building. A true temple

Humanity's Paradox

does not need bricks or mortar but water and blood. Our God dwells in humans especially in our heart and soul. Now this Last Supper you refer to is where Jesus along with his twelve apostles, gathered to initiate a new covenant.

God established the first covenant with Moses when God gave him the 10 – Commandments as a righteous way to live our lives. The first three commandments deal with a reverence for God followed by commandments for respect for life and honor to do what is right to live by. Now this Jesus, our Lord established the New Covenant of his body and blood for he tells us while at table he took the bread, said the blessing, broke it, and gave it to his apostles, saying,

"This is my body, which will be given for you;
do this in memory of me."
And likewise the cup after they had eaten, saying,
"This cup is the new covenant in my blood,
which will be shed for you." Lk 22:19-20

Luke concludes his letter by writing that I hope this letter finds you well and this gives you sufficient answers to your provocative questions on why we gather and partake of Jesus' body and blood.

Luke prays and reflects to himself that the human heart and mind that empowers society to do the unconscionable actions in life, do not live up to the standards set before us by Jesus' life and death.

A Believer

In the course of attending more gatherings and learning about prayer, worship, receiving the Body and Blood of Christ and opening the Word of God, Antipas' questions multiplied and just about overwhelmed Luke.

This notion of Baptism intrigues me, but I'm afraid I am totally oblivious as to it's meaning and concept, as the pertinent questions just flowed from Antipas to Luke.

Luke tries to respond to that poignant question the best way he can, by telling Antipas that even our Messiah, Jesus, found difficulty in explaining Baptism to Nicodemus, a Pharisee and ruler of the Jews.

Nicodemus came to Jesus one night and called him, Rabbi, and admitted that he indeed is a teacher who has come from God. For no one can do all the signs and miracles that Jesus performed, unless God is with him. Jesus answered and said to him, "Amen, amen, I say to you, no one can see the kingdom of God without being born from above."

Nicodemus' discombobulation went way beyond being confused and put the question to Jesus, "How can a person once grown old be born again? Surely, he cannot reenter his mother's womb and be born again, can he?"

Jesus answered, "Amen, amen I say to you, no one can enter the Kingdom of God without being born of water and Spirit." Jn 3:5

Then Luke continues to explain the words of Jesus as he spoke them to Nicodemus. No one has gone up to heaven except the one who has come down from heaven, the Son of Man. And just as Moses lifted up the serpent in the desert, so must the Son of Man be lifted up, so that everyone who believe in him may have eternal life.

Luke put his quill down, for his eyes are getting weary and rubs them to ease the weariness. He then again picks up his quill and continues to explain, "For God so loved the world that he gave his only Son, so that everyone who believes in him might not perish but might have eternal life." Jn 3:16

Luke stops his writing and contemplates the why's of eternity, and then continues writing to Antipas that long before the downfall of humanity in the garden of Eden, there was the downfall of the angels in heaven. A major battle pursued for the Glory of God's heaven and Satan along with a cohort of bad angels rebelled and from that point on are thrown out of heaven and become the demons of mankind.

Due to this major rebellion and downfall, Satan is a thorn in God's side forever, until the end of time. Now when God's creation of earth, life and humanity begins; we are created in God's image and given free will of choice to follow God or follow the temptations of Satan.

This Satan temps Adam and Eve and because of their failure, we have original sin. This Baptism of a spiritual rebirth, removes original sin and implants the gifts of the Holy Spirit to guide us in life so we may bare good fruit.

A Believer

Luke concludes his letter to Antipas with, it is getting late my new found friend in Christ, Peace be with you!

There were many such meetings of Christians at the gatherings of homes throughout Asia Minor and the known world from Rome to Athens and so forth. As the gatherings grew, baptisms became a choice amongst believers and the Word of God spread.

Antipas, inspired by these ceremonial baptisms, once again questions Luke, "What exactly happens to the person being baptized?"

Luke ponders how to answer that question and looks out his window to see children playing. Some are running, skipping but others are sitting on the ground writing in the dirt with a stick. When anyone makes a mistake on whatever they are writing or drawing, then they just wipe it clean with their hand and start anew. This gives an excellent example of wiping the slate clean and writes to Antipas,

My dear friend in Christ, Baptism is wiping the slate clean to start anew. For original sin planted in our soul at birth, from the beginning of the downfall of Adam and Eve is wiped clean through Baptism, our spiritual rebirth. Not only that but the gifts of the Holy Spirit are implanted in our soul to guide us in faith. From the holy gifts of the spirit, we receive knowledge, wisdom, understanding, council, piety, fear of the Lord and fortitude. What marvelous gifts from God! God's grace and blessings to help guide us through life.

The period of time of letter writing, delivery by scribe and waiting for a return reply could take a couple of months. By then there would be more questions and the process of query and answers would begin anew.

Antipas' excitement of being apart of something that seemed bigger than life and larger than the world itself was a monumental awakening for him and in his searching for meaning to life, asked many more questions.

Luke felt enthralled by his friend's eager questions but cautioned Antipas to take it one step at a time for the process of being a true believer is like a metamorphosis, a transformation that takes time. One must allow the spirit to work from within. And through prayer, worship, devotion, bible reading and almsgiving; the spiritual growth will take place. By the time Luke receives another letter form Antipas, another Gladiatorial bout has taken place. But now Antipas sees the futility in such games.

The next letter of Antipas takes both Luke and Antipas to the next spiritual level with the thought-provoking question, "Why the gifts of the Holy Spirit?"

Luke reflects on this question and remembers a story about Jesus and the barren fig tree and he told them this parable:

> "There once was a person who had a
> fig tree planted in his orchard,
> and when he came in search of
> fruit on it but found none,

> he said to the gardener, 'For three years now I have
> come in search of fruit on this fig
> tree but have found none.
> So, cut it down. Why should it exhaust the soil?'
> He said to him in reply, 'Sir, leave it for this year also,
> and I shall cultivate the ground around it and fertilize it;
> it may bear fruit in the future. If not,
> you can cut it down.' Lk 13:6-9

Now my good friend Antipas the moral of the story is this, Jesus Christ warns all Christians that they must bear fruit after their conversion from baptism worthy of repentance or risk being condemned. The gifts of the Holy Spirit are to be utilized to bear good fruit. But if there is no fruit, no repentance, God's patience will come to an end, and the fruitless, unrepentant individual will be cut down.

And of course, the next question from Antipas over the next few months was, 'what are the fruits that we must bear from the gifts of the Holy Spirit?'

Humanity's Paradox

Picture from Creative Commons

Gifts and Fruits of the Holy Spirit

- Gifts:
- Knowledge
- Understanding
- Wisdom
- Counsel
- Fear of the Lord
- Piety
- Fortitude

Fruits:
Love – Faithfulness
Joy – Gentleness
Peace
Patience
Kindness
Generosity
Self-Control

A Believer

Then Luke tells the parable that Jesus told of the 'Good Samaritan' to reinforce what are the fruits of the Holy Spirit.

There was a scholar of the law who stood up to test Jesus and said. "Teacher, what must I do to inherit eternal life?

Jesus replied, "What is written in the law? How do you read it?"

The scholar replied, "You shall love the Lord, your God, with all your heart, with all your being, with all your strength, and with all your mind, and your neighbor as yourself."

Jesus replied to him, "You have answered correctly; do this and you will live."

But because he wished to justify himself, he said to Jesus, "And who is my neighbor?"

Jesus replied, "A man fell victim to robbers as he went down from Jerusalem to Jericho. They stripped and beat him and went off leaving him half-dead.

A priest happened to be going down that road, but when he saw him, he passed by on the opposite side. Likewise, a Levite came to the place, and when he saw him, he passed by on the opposite side. But a Samaritan traveler who came upon him was moved with compassion at the sight. He approached the victim, poured oil and wine over his wounds and bandaged them. Then he lifted him up on his own animal, took him to an inn and cared for him. The next day he took out two silver coins and gave them to the innkeeper with the instructions, 'Take care of him. If you spend more than what I have given you, I shall repay you on my way back.'

Which of these three, in your opinion, was the neighbor to the robbers' victim?

He answered, "The one who treated him with mercy."

Jesus said to him, "Go and do likewise.'

Antipas is learning that life is a special gift from God. By utilizing our gifts from the Holy Spirit, each of us may transpire as a gift to others to care, help and share in their needs. To be truly a believer in Christ, is to do the Will of God.

Chapter 5

Antipas' Conversion

*Trust in the Lord with all of your heart,
on your own intelligence rely not;
In all your ways be mindful of him, and
he will make straight your paths.*
Proverbs 3:5-6

Another letter from Luke arrives for Antipas with a few words of advice. The timing couldn't have been any better, for he had just come from a gathering of Christians at Antonius' house and the discussion coincided with the monograph on the cross of Christ. His letter read about the conditions of discipleship.

"If anyone wishes to come after Jesus, he must deny himself and take up his cross daily and follow him. For whoever wishes to save his life will lose it, but whoever loses his life for my sake will save it. What profit is there for one to gain the whole world yet lose or forfeit himself? Whoever is ashamed of me and of my words, the Son of Man will be ashamed of when he comes in his glory and in the glory of the Father and of the holy angels. Truly I say to you, there are some standing here who will not taste death until they see the kingdom of God." Lk 9:23-27

Have you ever been to a friend's house and invited to stay for supper? The family sits at the table and says grace. Then a marvelous thing happens. The conversation just flows throughout supper. No bickering, or infighting, just pleasant conversion. Even if one disagrees with the topic, the various perspectives are presented and accepted by all. Marvelous, simply marvelous! And that is why Jesus invites all to sit at his table, the banquet of plenty, to receive his body and his blood. Each of us receives the totality of Jesus in Word, Body, Blood and Spirit. The only thing each of us must do, is to choose to sit at his table!

God loves diversity, after all, He created each of us in His image! All lives matter before God. But God so loved the world that he drew the line when it comes to His only begotten Son. Follow him and you will receive eternal life. This is the eternal message and this is the Will of God and He is the Alpha and the Omega.

Antipas is growing spiritually. An awakening that is a transition of accepting, acknowledging, acting and adoring. The first and most important step is to make

A Believer

the decision to follow God through Christ His Son, our Lord.

The gatherings have been a wake-up call for Antipas and Luke's letters, a mind-boggling learning experience. Now through the steps of baptism, eating the body and drinking the blood of Jesus to accept the new covenant, the Holy Spirit nurtures the Soul.

As Christians they come together, to worship, receive the body and blood of Christ, to listen to His Word and Will, and to give praise to our God through Jesus Christ, our Lord, Savior and High Priest. There is one thing that all of us can be reassured in and that is something that St. Paul wrote to the Romans, "We know that all things work together for the good of those who love God, who are called according to his purpose. Rm 8:28

After attending a number of gatherings, Antipas became extremely perplexed. And so, he writes to his new found friend Luke and basically empties his feelings about these gatherings, worship, prayer and the very people that attend these gatherings. The first letter chides the attendees about gossiping too much. The second letter points to how these sinners in their every day life come together to give worship and yet continue to sin? By the third letter Antipas is frustrated enough to recommend to Luke that he wants to stop attending the gatherings.

Luke learned from some of the original Apostles and from Paul who was blinded by our risen Lord to

Humanity's Paradox

see, hear and feel with his heart and soul. He turns to kneel and pray, reflect and contemplate on his next letter to Antipas. The sun has set before Luke arose from his prayer and put quill to paper and wrote these very words,

My dear friend, Antipas, we are all sinners and that is why God, our Heavenly Father sent his only begotten son to show us the way, be our light in a dark world, and be our unblemished lamb to die for us! When Jesus died, he descended to hell to let Satan known that his time had come and then arose from the dead. Through his resurrection, Jesus proved to the world that he overcame both sin and death. His ascension was witnessed by many and through the descent of the Holy Spirit, the gifts of the Holy Spirit are distributed to establish the Holy Church. Now before you make any major decisions about leaving the gathering, I will give you one last set of instructions through Antonius for your next gathering. Peace be with you my friend and always remember that God chose you and now it is your choice to choose Him.

And sure enough, within the next three gatherings, Antonius received the instructions from Luke which were to be given to Antipas. The instructions were simple with three direct questions to be asked of Antipas by Antonius. The instructions on the parchment read, 'Take a small bowl and fill it to the rim with water. Next, walk around the house of the gathering with the bowl of water without spilling any water.'

A Believer

So, with a frown on his face, Antipas filled a small bowl with water, that was provided to him by Antonius. He then proceeded outside and walked around the house of Antonius slowly so not to spill any water. Upon returning inside the house, Antonius asked three questions of Antipas:

1. Did you spill any water?

The reply from Antipas was no.

2. Why not?

Antipas replied that he was extremely focused on the bowl so not to spill any water.

3. Did you notice anyone gossiping or sinning?

Antipas reflected on the question before giving a reply of, 'no.'

Now Antonius has a short letter for Antipas from Luke which reads, "My dear friend Antipas, I was hoping that your reply to the third question would be no. For you see in order to carry the bowl without spilling any of it, you had to concentrate on your action. You were extremely focused on the bowl. Now when you come to the gathering which we call church, focus on your worship of God and you will not be distracted by others.

We Christians come to worship God and we do this by following His Son, our Lord and Redeemer, Jesus Christ.

From that point on, Antipas remained vigilant and continued to attend the gatherings.

Luke understood all too well, the purpose of church, the coming together in prayer, worship, hearing the Word of God and receiving the body and blood of the new covenant, Jesus Christ. Because Christians have found a common life as followers of Christ to be more important than their cultural differences. Also, he remembers the words of Jesus written by John in the Gospel about the murmurings of many of his disciples.

Many of Jesus' disciples who listened to him said, "Many of your sayings are difficult, who can accept them?"

Since Jesus knew that his disciples were murmuring about this, he asked them, "Does this shock you?"

After a brief moment of silence, Jesus said, "What if you were to see the Son of Man ascending to where he was before? It is the spirit that gives life, while the flesh is of no avail. The words I have spoken to you are Spirit and life. But there are some of you who do not believe."

Jesus knew from the beginning the ones who would not believe and the one who would betray him. And he said,

"For this reason, I have told you that no one can come to me unless it is granted him by my Father."

A Believer

As a result of this, many of his disciples returned to their former way of life and no longer accompanied him.

Jesus then said to the Twelve, "Do you also want to leave?"

It was Simon Peter who answered him, "Master, to whom shall we go! You have the words of eternal life. We have come to believe and are convinced that you are the Holy One of God."

It was also Simon Peter who relayed this story to Luke, for Luke was not one of the original twelve. Peter understood all too well, that Jesus is the Messiah, the one to follow to our Heavenly Father but the evil that exists in our world expands exponentially to the sins of the people and Peter wasn't prepared for that. For the thorn in God's side is our antagonist, the devil; be soberminded; be watchful for our adversary because the devil prowls around liked a roaring lion, seeking someone to devour. Be firm in your faith, resist him, knowing that the same kinds of suffering are being experienced by all of humanity throughout the world. 1Pt 5:8-9

Peter reminded Luke to remember the words of Jesus which were spoken to the original apostles, "What profit is there for one to gain the whole world and forfeit his life? What could one give in exchange for his life? Whoever is ashamed of me and of my words in this faithless and sinful generation, the Son of Man will be ashamed of that person when he comes in his glory with the holy angels.

Life is a precious gift from God, but he never promised that it would be easy! Why is that? Because God has already set the stage of creation for eternal life. First in heaven, then on earth before the foundation of time. His omnipotence was revealed to Adam and Eve and the beginning of humanity. And what happened? Disobedience of Adam and Eve, the killing of Cain, and the spread of sinfulness. When the Lord saw how great was man's wickedness on earth, and how no desire that his heart conceived was ever anything but evil, he regretted that he had ever made man on the earth, and his heart was grieved.

God at that point in our lives decided enough is enough and preparation for the flood takes place. We must all remember that God was first disobeyed by the angels and now he is disobeyed by humanity. The great flood takes place and we all know about the story of Noah and the Ark.

God's love triumph's again, when he again reveals himself to the patriarchs and establishes his people. The testing of Abraham with his young son to prove his love for God. The descendants flourish but abominations exist and God intervenes again. We know about the story of Sodom and Gomorrah and humanity should have learned how to remain faithful before God.

Generations flourished, but so to did the sins of pride, covetousness, lust, anger, gluttony, envy and sloth. And again, God must come to the rescue of his people from the Egyptians and establishes the first covenant on Mount Sinai with Moses.

Time marches on from eons to millenniums, from centuries to generations and with the Lord one day is as a thousand years, and a thousand years as one day. 2Pt 3:8

God so loved the world that he sent his only begotten Son, that whoever should believe in him might have eternal life. Jn 3:16

Yes, God sent his Son to reveal his love again! To show us the way and be our unblemished lamb to die for us. Our Lord, Jesus Christ arose from the dead to prove that he had overcome both sin and death. He ascended to Heaven! But God did not leave us as orphans and we have the descent of the Holy Spirit to establish the Holy Church. And the Holy Church is the life saving vessel today through the waters of baptism, as Noah's Ark was the lifesaving vessel back then through the floodwaters. But again, many abominations exist before the eyes of God.

Antipas is beginning to realize that and as he attends many more gatherings of Christians, he meets many people of diverse backgrounds. People of the elite and nobility did not rub elbows with the lower classes. That is one of the miraculous functions of church, we are all children of God. Barriers are removed, respect is established and each brings a reverence for God to worship. One such person that Antipas associates with is Demetrius, an outspoken stonemason from one of the trades. In due time their friendship grows and as Antipas reads the monographs from Luke to the gathering, his comments are priceless.

Demetrius asked the question that if Christ is the cornerstone of the church, then he was a stonemason, right?

Interpretations are in the mind of the beholder, right?

Many questions arose from the assembly of people as to Luke's title of Christ as the 'Son of Man.' Most were dumbfounded as to the meaning of the term and beckoned Antipas to write to Luke on this comment in his letter. So, we find Antipas the very next day putting quill to parchment and asking Luke the significance of the term, 'Son of Man.'

This becomes a difficult proposition for Luke as he contemplates his answer. He remembers all too well, the pain of Mary when speaking to her. The mother of our Lord witnessed and understood better than anyone else the terms, 'Son of Man' and 'Son of God.' But how she came to understand those terms caused her much pain.

Luke struggles as he puts quill to parchment and writes to Antipas what becomes the beginning chapters of his Gospel. The angel of the Lord, Gabriel, announces to Mary that she is to become the mother of our Lord. Hence the term, 'Son of God' refers to the deity of Christ. When the term 'Son of Man' is used as a title it refers to the humanity of Jesus Christ.

A Believer

'Son of Man' reminds everyone, believers and nonbelievers that Jesus became a man so that He could die for us. 'Son of God reminds us that Jesus is God so that He could live a sinless life and be the perfect sacrificial Lamb of God. Only as the God-man could He die a sinless, holy sacrifice for our sins. All that is left for us is to believe and walk by faith and not by sight!

This dying for us was extremely painful for both God in Heaven and Mary at the foot of the cross. As Mary gazed upward towards her suffering son, the tears from her heart caused ripples in her soul and it was felt by God in Heaven.

Christ came at a time in history when the miscreants, misery and hardships culminated at a nadir of life. Add to this the chaos of enduring wars, abuse, and endless taxations and the endless persecutions of life seemed insurmountable. Then comes along Christianity which offers an alternative to the dearth of life. God is real through Jesus Christ. You can speak to Him through prayer, worship and loving your neighbor. This is a time when the elite were few and the many were destitute. From the beginning of time to the very threshold of the second coming the words of Charles Dickens rings so true,

"It was the age of wisdom, it was the age of foolishness,
It was the epoch of belief, it was
the epoch of incredulity,
It was the season of light, it was the season of darkness,
It was the spring of hope, it was the winter of despair."

God's redeeming love is Jesus Christ, our final hope in a tumultuous world of despondency!

Luke concludes his monograph with tears in eyes and pain in his heart with the words of Jesus to console Antipas, "No one can serve two masters. You cannot serve both God and money," and then wishes Antipas God speed. He then gives his letter to Stachys, Antipas' faithful servant, for delivery to Antipas. Stachys has patiently been waiting for three days for the reply letter to the questions of the gathering and of his master, Antipas.

Stachys was one of the fortunate ones, for even though he was a servant and what many would consider a lower class, he was treated well and had no wants or fears. Upon receiving the reply letter, Antipas eagerly reads the monograph and sits back to reflect on the words. He ponders that there is much more to this Christianity then meets the eye; for the rudiments of faith have to pierce the soul as the lance of the Roman soldier pierced the heart of Jesus.

Antipas sits back in his chair and looks out his window towards the meadows and streams of running water. He sees the birds in the sky and the trees and flowers in full bloom. He discerns his affluence and position as a member of the elite, Roman citizenship and wonders, can I become a true Christian? This dilemma perplexes Antipas and he realizes that choices in his life have to be made.

A Believer

It is difficult to image of being the Son of God and yet possess such humbleness as to serve others as Jesus did in the healing, teaching, and miracles performed. Most leaders within the world demonstrate a status of honor, power and prestige and now comes this Jesus of forgiveness, sacrifice and divine mercy. Antipas falls to his knees, and thinks to himself, 'Wow, wow, Amen.'

From that point on in his life, changes take place, Antipas transitions from a spectator to a champion to persevere for God. He was an excellent organizer for the gladiatorial games, why not focus his talents for the gatherings to benefit the church and its members. Collections were taken each week to benefit the needy. Between the infirm, homeless and destitute there are many needs beyond the collections. Distribution of supplies, the placement for jobs, shelter and the needs of medical attention required many hands. Through church, almsgiving is a way of life to help others.

There was one such case that Antipas took a personal interest. There was a young girl by the name of Nouna, about seven years in age with brilliant eyes and a beautiful smile who was found wandering in the city. Apparently, her parents abandoned her for whatever reason and she was alone, afraid and lost. Thank God there are chaperons from the church that reconnoiter the city to help those in need.

Ruf and his wife took the child in until a permanent home could be found for her. Antipas enjoyed playing with her and looked forward to his visits at their home. Having the means to help out, he provided the necessary means for clothes, supplies and whatever she needed. For the very words of Jesus must ring out in our heart and soul, love God with your whole heart and your neighbor as yourself. In any plain language that means get off your sorrowful butt and help! For what most people value highly in this life, is detestable in Almighty God's sight! The good Samaritan did not walk by a person in need as others turned a blind eye. Love of God and your neighbor is paramount in this life to ever get to eternal life! In this life the bridges of friendship are invaluable because it is a trust and bond that never can be broken. The bond of the love of God in our soul and Christ in our heart consummates our perfection in life for without God we are an empty vessel. The bonds of friendship between Luke and Antipas were quintessential due to their common bond of love of God through Jesus Christ.

Antipas writes to Luke who is staying at Calpurnius house, that he plans to leave Pergamum for a few months and return to his homeland in Caesarea and visit with his son. He would like to board a ship in Ephesus bound for Caesarea and by chance if Luke was available to meet face to face. The bonds of friendship with an actual meeting would solidify then their mere pen pal relationship. Most of your readings are received well and I now understand why Theophilus conscripted you to write a Gospel for the Gentiles. Although there are parts of the Gospel that are difficult to understand for Christianity is a new mind set and one must open their heart and soul as well as their mind to begin to comprehend God's love through Jesus Christ for us.

On a different note, the concept of the greatest commandment of loving God with your whole heart is not one that is difficult to accept, but love of neighbor as yourself is something else! I for one know many obnoxious neighbors that I would rather shoot then love. Oh well, it takes time for the ethereal to settle in the heart and soul because it seems so surreal at times. Living in a very real physical world and striving to live the spiritual ideals is a mission impossible for many of us. I hope this letter finds you well and in time for a joyous meeting and then signed the letter and quickly gave it to his scribe to deliver.

Prior to his leaving, Antipas decided to slash the Gordian knot and facilitate the arrangements for the little girl Nouna to be adopted by his new friend Demetrius and his wife Diotis whom Nouna has grown very fond of. Having the necessary means, wealth and connections, Antipas provided a lifetime income for them to rear the child as one of their own. Since too they fell in love with the girl and were barren, Antipas became their benefactor and made sure all the 'i's' were dotted and all the 't's' were crossed so that the arrangements would be for the betterment of both parties. She should live a happy life under their oversight of love and unaware of my benefaction.

The musical romp of life has taken place with each new generation from the beginning of time and that journey is so fleeting. The purpose of life is to know and love God, follow his divine Son and utilize the gifts of the Holy Spirit to do good. Antipas was beginning to realize this and it overcame him like a gentle breeze from the Aegean Sea and he wept. He was boarding one of the freighters bound for Caesarea and had just completed a two-day visit with Luke. Their first meeting was prodigious for Luke helped Antipas in many ways. He helped Antipas to unlock an intellect to understand God, a reason to discern him, diligence to seek him, a spirit to know him, wisdom to find him and an open heart to meditate upon him. May each of us have ears to hear him, our eyes to behold him, a heart to love him and our tongue to proclaim him. It was a good journey to Caesarea.

Our faith helps us overcome the rigors of life. The harsh severities of catastrophic storms, war, pestilence and famine. Faith makes us survivable to overcome and persevere through the hard times and never forget that God is always in charge of our lives.

Antipas walked along the promenade deck to the bow of the ship to view their departure. Many ships were commuting to-and-fro from all ports of the Mediterranean Sea. Ephesus was a commercial hub and

A Believer

the most important trading center in the Mediterranean region. Throughout history, Ephesus survived multiple attacks and changed hands many times between conquerors.

The refreshing, salty sea air was invigorating for Antipas as he looked forward to seeing his son and family in Caesarea again. He reflected over his life and how Christianity is beginning to change his perspective on life. His conscience was awakened to the disparity of life between the upper class of nobility and elite from the lower classes of peasants, merchants and artisans. The elite have no worries or wants for it is all at their beckoning. The elite enjoy a lavish, extravagant lifestyle, while the majority of the peasants strive in a meager existence. As the old adage goes, 'the rich get richer and the poor get poorer.'

The two extreme lifestyles that were diametrically opposed prompted Antipas to consider making some changes in his lifestyle when he gets back home to Pergamum. The words of Jesus were often harsh and critical of the practices and values of the elite towards the downtrodden. His sermon on the Mount proclaimed the Kingdom of God and the belief in one's final accountability before God. As he looked out across the vastness of the sea and reflected on the tumultuous times, the thoughts of Luke's writings about Christ calming the sea came to his mind.

Humanity's Paradox

Picture from Creative Commons

Antipas shook his head and thought to himself, 'If only life could be that easy!'

But God requires us to take the initiative to do right, and at that pinnacle moment, Antipas understood his next choices in life.

First, upon his return to Pergamum he would relinquish his position to work on the next gladiatorial games for the display of torture, fights and killings are an abomination to Almighty God. Secondly, establish Demetrius and Diotis as the permanent guardians of

A Believer

Nouna with a lifelong financial assistance. And third, pursue the quality time to study Luke's monographs to learn and now follow this person by the name of Jesus Christ, our Messiah and Lord.

Revelations to inspire may only happen once in a lifetime and for Antipas this was his time. Upon his return after visiting with his son and family which was a joyous occasion, Antipas was committed to adhere to his convictions. Those inner feelings that speak to the soul and heart that this must be done. The impetus of course coming from God and the Holy Spirit through our very soul and heart. That is why Jesus teaches us the most important prayer to pray at the sermon on the Mount,

> "Our Father who art in heaven,
> Hallowed be your name,
> your kingdom come,
> your will be done,
> on earth as in heaven.
> Give us this day our daily bread;
> and forgive us our debts,
> as we forgive our debtors;
> and do not subject us to the final test,
> but deliver us from evil." Amen!

The gatherings, the church of souls, is our recharging, revitalization to persevere in faith. God gives us the gift of life, his Divine Son of expiation to follow, and in-turn we give Him worship and reverence through His Son.

Luke has forwarded the last monograph to Antipas about Jesus and it is riveting to say the least. The monograph depicts the agony and passion of our Lord. From the agony in the Garden of Gethsemane, the scourging at the pillar, the carrying of His cross, to His crucifixion. Antipas reads the last monograph and as he gets into some of the paragraphs, he has to put it down. The horror depicted of the severe scourging by the Roman soldiers of Jesus with a flagellum was more than Antipas could understand or bear. There was no limit to the number of lashings even to the extent of ripping the flesh down to the bones. No wonder Jesus needed help in carrying his cross.

The difficulty in understanding God's love is that all the nuances of Jesus's life is for us. The nativity, born to make visible what was invisible to us. Both the shepherds and Magi understood that. The finding in the Temple where the teachers were all amazed at the understanding and wisdom of Jesus at the age of twelve. For he had the wisdom of God. The baptism which Jesus, the Son of God, did not need but to prove how vital for the spiritual rebirth, Jesus was baptized by John the Baptist. This is paramount for the beginning of our spiritual journey. The self-manifestation at the wedding of Cana, the first miracle performed, to many more miracles, healings and teachings for us to learn about God's love. The passion,

A Believer

death, resurrection and ascension to reveal the glory of God. All for us!

Does anyone really understand the divine mercy of redemption? Because if you do, then you should humble yourself, get on your knees and pray to God! Thanks be to God; we have eternal life through Jesus Christ.

Antipas was beginning to realize this in a profound way. The more he went to the gatherings, the more he grew in spirit. And the more he grew in spirit, the illumination by the spirit blossomed from within. His feelings seemed to synthesize on wisdom of God, love of neighbor and meaning of what is the purpose of life. As Christ called the apostles, each of us are to become apostles and spread the Word of God. The Word of God is His will be done.

His fondness of neighbor transpired into love of neighbor and not only of those that were close associates but the poor, destitute and infirm. Why should one love only those that you know but what about the slave, those in prison and the sick? Should we not pray and acknowledge them as our brothers and sisters of God? Are we all created in God's image? Life took an about-face, a one-hundred and eighty degrees turn and Antipas made more of his wealth available for the less fortunate. His involvement at the gatherings intensified, and his love of neighbor became real. Shelters for the homeless were built, food for the hungry provided and means of medical care provided for the infirm became a common place from the various churches.

Antipas had the political pull, wealth and finesse to get things done and wasted no time of doing just that. He allowed himself one luxury in life and that was to enjoy time with Nouna, who grew in spirit and blossomed into a lovely young girl. Demetrius and Diotis also burgeoned in love and happiness for Nouna and the epitome of family life became real for the both of them. But always behind the sunshine eventually follows a cloudy-rainy day.

Antipas certainly had his effects on Nouna but also influenced Demetrius' convictions about his faith. Now the boastful stonemason had a new perspective on life. When one makes Jesus Christ the center of your life, spontaneous changes take place and before one knows it, the bubble of life will burst because we exist in an ungodly world. That tug of war between good and evil is always prevalent.

One evening as Antipas and Demetrius were returning from the Emporium, their eyes noticed the sign of the fish over the door mantel of Ignatius' house. There was another impromptu gathering taken place and so both Antipas and Demetrius decided to attend. While there they learned of another manuscript that recounts the life of Jesus of Nazareth. But this manuscript was written by a man named Matthew. Unlike Luke, this Matthew was one of the original twelve apostles and knew Jesus well. As they listened intently to the writings of Matthew, there was one particular passage that enlighten their heart and soul. Demetrius was transfixed in his seat as Ignatius read the words,

"When the Son of Man comes in his glory, and all the angels with him, he will sit on his glorious throne. All the nations will be gathered before him, and he will separate the people one from another as a shepherd separates the sheep from the goats. He will put the sheep on his right and the goats on his left.

Then the King will say to those on his right, 'Come, you who are blessed by my Father; take your inheritance, the kingdom prepared for you since the creation of the world. For I was hungry and you gave me something to eat. I was thirsty and you gave me something to drink. I was a stranger and you invited me in. I needed clothes and you clothed me. I was sick and you looked after me. I was in prison and you came to visit me.'

Then the righteous will answer him, 'Lord, when did we see you hungry and feed you, or thirsty and give you something to drink? When did we see you as a stranger and invite you in, or needing clothes and clothe you? When did we see you sick or in prison and go to visit you?'

The King will reply, 'Truly I tell you, whatever you did for one of the least of the brothers and sisters of mine, you did for me.'" Mt. 25:31-40

These words became embedded into the hearts of both Antipas and Demetrius and became the instrument of their new found hope. As time progressed, any Christian at any one of the gatherings became an enemy to the empire. The authorities in Rome suspected all Christians as antisocial miscreants and an enemy to Caesar. All subjects of the Roman Empire should give homage to Caesar and Caesar alone. This became an affront to his Christian duty and Demetrius confronted anyone, including the Roman authority that said otherwise!

Need I say anymore? Demetrius was arrested, put in chains, and sequestered under prison guards in a remote dungeon. His lovely wife and stepdaughter had to be cared for at Antonius house and could not even visit him for the Roman guards would not reveal his where-abouts.

The isolation affected all three of them. In the weeks to follow, Diotis lost weight, became gaunt and despair set in. The bright-eyed, beautiful Nouna who had blossomed like a sunflower became despondent and saddened to daily tears. The thought of not seeing her step dad, Demetrius again, impaired her to become a mute. And Demetrius himself, was at the very precipice of his life. For you see the precipice of life is death.

God gave us the gift of life in his image. Each of us have a lifetime to acknowledge, accept and believe in Our Heavenly Father. Once we understand that, then and only then, can we follow His divine Son and give the proper worship, devotion and prayers. When we come to

A Believer

this critical juncture in our life, there is no turning back for we are warned, "Do not conform yourselves to this age but be transformed by the renewal of your mind, that you may discern what is the will of God, what is good, pleasing and perfect." Rom. 12:2

Demetrius renewed with the strength of Jesus went to a corner of his cell, kneeled, prayed and remembered the verses about the Agony in the Garden of Gethsemane where Jesus removed himself from his apostles to pray alone to his Heavenly Father. He prayed for the wisdom from God to lead him and the courage of Christ to persevere to a holy death.

The following day he was brought before the civic authorities, and before the seal of the Roman emperor, asked to retract his subversive claims that Jesus Christ is our sole Lord and ruler, Amen.

Renewed by his faith, Demetrius could not do this! The officials castigated him as an antagonist against the Roman Empire and an antisocial miscreant against the Roman Emperor. He was sentenced to death and waits for the next gladiatorial games where he will be executed by one of the demented tortures that will be prescribed by the emperor.

Those weeks seemed like years in a cold, dark, rat-infested, foul-smelling cell. No windows to see the daylight, or even aware of each passing day. Just endless darkness to cloud his mind and numb his senses. The only comfort for him was his prayers. The smell from the rats nibbling at his toes, and the pungent odor from his feces and urine was unbearable. But in Demetrius' mind, Jesus' life challenged all evil in this life, his death absorbed them; his resurrection defeated them and his ascension glorified His Heavenly Father.

The day before the gladiatorial games in which Emperor Domitian would attend, Demetrius was taken to the public baths to clean himself, given a new set of clothes and a meal fit for a king. That evening he was allowed sleeping quarters in chambers fit for nobility. No rats, no foul-smelling odors, and a balcony that overlooked the panoramic view of the city.

The first day of the gladiatorial debut, Demetrius was awakened early and taken to the amphitheater by way of the underground tunnel to be prepared for his execution. There were primarily eight main divisions in the day-long events.

- Parade of beasts that were to devour their victims
- Staged battles
- Four gladiatorial games of Elite
- Heavily armed
- Lightly armed
- Unusually exotic
- Throwing Christians to the lions
- Executions

A Believer

These gladiatorial events throughout the Roman Empire were their gargantuan escapades like our Superbowl and Stanley Cup playoffs. It normally begins with much fanfare, music, appearance of the emperor, parade of the gladiators, criminals and beast from lions, tigers, bears and even elephants. Crude devices were invented for the spectacle of executions and were paraded around the arena as a warning and deterrent for all spectators. It was all very over-whelming for Demetrius who was lost to his own thoughts and prayers. The various executions were the last events on the agenda and Demetrius had to wait in his cage impatiently until he was hauled to the center of the arena. The large crowds would stand and cheer as those who were led out to be executed were led to stand before the emperor.

One spectator, from the far side of the arena, enters through the attendant's gate unimpeded. He walks at a brisk pace to the side of the arena where the emperor is seated. Once there, he looks up towards the emperor's box and with a clear and sharp voice proclaims, "Hail Domitian, emperor of Rome."

The imperial guards rushed in to overtake this perpetrator but the emperor arose from his seat and raised his arms to quiet the crowd and stop the imperial guards from arresting this pretentious intruder. His curiosity peeked; Domitian was amused to see why this person had the audacity to approach the emperor.

Once silence was regained from the crowd, the perpetrator again began to speak, "Hail Domitian, gracious emperor of Rome, I am Antipas, a nobleman of this great empire. I have found much favor in my birth, business and status in the cities of Tyre, Caesarea, Ephesus and most recently Pergamum. I have been a great benefactor to the Pax Romana, peace brought about by Rome, by way of endowments to library's, monuments and most recently a statue of your greatness to the entrance of this great city of Pergamum. Indeed, I laid the ground work for the gladiatorial events such as these. But my heart, loyalty and passion has been ignited by another, this Jesus Christ of Nazareth, who died for all so sins could be forgiven. Yes, I joined the 'Gatherings' and give worship to the one and true God who sent His Son to show us the way! And forgive my boldness, but this Demetrius whom you are about to execute is innocent of any wrong doings for you see," just then, Antipas turns and looks around the arena at the throng of spectators and sees that his words have an effect on all. Again, Antipas looks up at the emperor and defiantly tells him that, "As the captain of a ship gives orders to the helmsman, if the ship runs aground, then it is the captain of the ship who is held liable. Then it is I who led Demetrius to the gatherings and influenced him to trust in the One True God and His Son, Jesus Christ! So, you see your excellency, that it is I who should hold the blame and not Demetrius. Show your benevolence and

A Believer

wise judgement by allowing me to take Demetrius' place of execution and allow him to be free."

The spectators looked on in total disbelief that anyone should want to take the place of another at an execution. The silence was deafening as the crowd eagerly waited for the emperor's decision. Domitian in reflection rubbed his jaw with his right hand and then rose to address the crowd. Raising both of his arms to proclaim his decision he said, "I, Emperor Domitian, will leave this decision to release Demetrius, to the citizens of this great empire and in-turn execute you Antipas if they so desire."

Just then the entire assembly at the arena arose and gave a thumbs-up to release Demetrius. The imperial guards quickly escorted Demetrius from the gladiatorial arena as Antipas was bound in chains and led to the center of the arena.

A Chianina bull, one of the oldest purebred bovine breeds, was led out from the side stalls to the center where Antipas stood. The bull was quickly killed by the thrust of a lance, gutted, emptied of its entrails and poor Antipas was thrust into the empty cavity of the bull and bound in by chains wrapped around the bull.

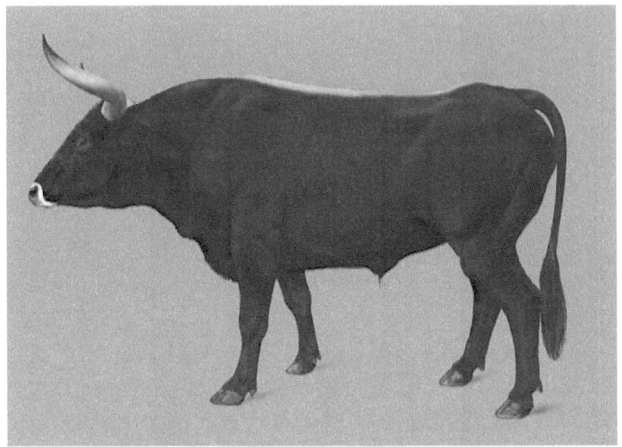

Picture from Creative Commons

A huge bond fire was made with soaked timbers of wine and the bull with Antipas inside, suspended over the fire. The searing of the flesh of both the bull and Antipas permeated the air. As the intensity of the flames were stoked, and as painful as the scorching heat penetrated Antipas body, not one utterance of a sound could be heard. No agonizing screams, for Antipas was deep in prayer with one thought in his mind, a deep love in his heart and a sincere beckoning in his soul, "Take me oh Lord, for I am a worthless sinner who loves thee above all things." Amen.

Demetrius is now in the embrace of his loving wife and stepdaughter. He makes an unyielding resolution; that someday he will have to reveal the true benefactor of Antipas to Nouna.

Chapter 6

The Wrath of God

The beginning of Christianity flourished from a dystopian society of the Roman Empire; an era that persecuted, tortured and condemned to death those who followed the Messiah, our Lord, Jesus Christ.

Thanks be to God for His Agape love, a love so pure, a love that creates, nourishes and is trueful; this is the love of God. From this love comes the gift of life, sustenance and purpose. Our Loving Father always provides gifts to each of His children, as part of their daily sustenance, from the moment they are conceived, until eternity. The gifts that He provides to us are those things which we receive from Him, without exerting any effort to receive them. Then his ultimate love sends His only begotten Son to die for our sins and gain us redemption.

For by grace, you have been saved through faith, and this is not from you; it is the gift of God; it is not from your works, so no one can boast. For we are his handiwork, created in Christ Jesus for the good works that God has prepared in advance, that we should live in them. Eph 2:8-10

Remember this, doing the will of God from the heart, willingly serving the Lord and not human beings, knowing full well that each will be requited from the Lord for whatever good you do. Put on the armor of God so that you may be able to stand firm against the tactics of the devil.

We are given special gifts from God through the Holy Spirit and these gifts are a special grace to help us practice virtue more perfectly. The gift of wisdom for example is a gift of knowledge that allows us to understand God's divine will. But here again a believer must utilize the spiritual fabric of faith in prayer, worship, devotion, bible reading and almsgiving and we will bear fruit! Almsgiving you say, why almsgiving? Because God's Will simply put, wants us to help our unfortunate neighbor. Remember when Jesus is asked, "what is the greatest commandment?"

And Jesus replies to love God with your whole heart and soul and to love your neighbor as yourself.

So, each of us must ask ourselves, am I going to listen to the Word and Will of God or am I going to shun His Will and follow the whims of temptation.

This is a paramount moment in each of our lives because the wrath of God is real! It is not about if it may happen, but when? Paul speaks about the day of judgement as the "day of wrath." Rm 2:5

Jesus Christ, whom God sent to die for us as our propitiation, says about God's wrath, "Woe to you." Mt 3:7

The very last book of the Holy Bible, Revelation refers to both, "the wrath of the Lamb" and "the wrath of the Almighty God." Rev 6:16; 19:15

The whole Bible story leads to a day when God will deal with all evil fully, finally, and forever. "Respice finem," consider the end. Sound advice for all because "Alea iacta est," the die is cast. This will be the day of wrath, when God will recompense every evil and bring to judgement every sin. Once the day of God's wrath will come, then the door of grace will be closed. The scales of God's benevolence with His agape love on one side and His wrath to banish evil on the other side is a reality of the coming judgement.

God will do this in perfect justice and the punishment for all sins will match our transgressions. God will send His only begotten Son who died for all and in the second coming will judge all. Then God will usher in a new heaven which will be home of righteousness. The anger of God is not something that resides in him by nature. It is a response to evil and sin. For it is provoked by the very abominations of our sins.

But our Heavenly Father's wrath is paramount, it is his holy response to the intrusion of evil into his world.

If and this is a big if, there was no sin in the world, then there would be no wrath in God. But remember before the downfall of humanity, there was the downfall of the angels and this all occurred before the foundation of the world. God holds out the offer of grace and forgiveness through Jesus Christ, our Lord and Savior. 2Pt 3:9

Humanity from the beginning of time has always been too complacent to listen to God! Look at what happened to Adam and Eve and the banishment from the garden of Eden. And most are too apathetic to do God's Will! When it comes to God's wrath, it is transparent and very volatile. God's wrath on the individual is disheartening such as the banishment of Cain for killing his brother Abel compared to the incapacitating wrath such as the great flood during Noah's time or the fire and brimstone of Sodom and Gomorrah. From the Ten Plagues of Egypt to the seven bowls of God's wrath found in Revelation, these are horrific consequences to the abominations of horrific sins.

Sodom and Gomorrah

The Seven Bowls of God's Wrath in Revelation

Pictures from Creative Commons

Whether from an individual or the multitude their insolence and ambivalence do not win favor with God's will! Believers shall not fear! The wrath of God is for those that do not believe and for those who do not do the will of God. For in Romans 1:18 the Bible tells us, "For the wrath of God is revealed from heaven against all ungodliness and unrighteousness of all, who hold the truth in unrighteousness," and in John3:36, "Whoever believes in the Son has eternal life, but whoever disobeys the Son will not see life, but the wrath of God remains on them."

There is a further warning in the book of Romans 2:5 which states that because of your stubbornness and unrepentant heart you are storing up wrath for yourself in the day of wrath and revelation of the righteous judgement of God.

God the Creator of all has not destined us for wrath but for acquiring salvation through our Lord Jesus Christ. 1 Thessalonians 5:9

God is perfectly just. Jesus our Lord is unblemished, that is without sin and so when he is born of the Virgin Mary through the Holy Spirit and at the age of thirty begins his public ministry what does he do first? He is baptized by John the Baptist in the Jordan River. Why you may ask that one that doesn't know sin needs to be baptized? This is paramount for our spiritual beginning to wipe away original sin and so Jesus submits to the cleansing to show us the way to God. Think about that, infact, humble ourselves to pray, worship and give devotion for we can "flee from the wrath to come." Mt 3:7

Each one of us by being baptized into Jesus' justifying death and by living our Baptisms show the world that we accept that Jesus on Calvary took our punishment on Himself. "Now that we have been justified by His blood, we shall be saved by Him from God's wrath." Rm 5:9

However, if we don't live according to our Baptisms and continue to disobey God, then Jesus' justifying death is in vain for us. As Jesus has warned all of us, do not harden your hearts today because impenitent hearts refuse to repent their sins. Therefore, humble yourselves knowing that God so loved the world that He sacrificed His only begotten Son. Live your Baptism, obey the Lord and go to confession to repent your sins.

The words in Revelation 14:19 are sobering words that, "The angel swung his sickle on the earth, gathered its grapes and threw them into the great winepress of God's wrath. The grapes being the impenitent sinners and the great winepress, the un-consuming fires of Gehenna! Heaven is very real and so are the fiery pits of hell; the choice is yours where you will be going!

In plain English, God's wrath is His passion to set things right. St Paul's words ring so true throughout the ages no matter what the age may be, "Do not conform to the pattern of this world." Rm 12:1-2

Humanity's Paradox

God certainly does not have to beg our pardon, because since the fall of Adam and Eve in the garden of Eden, God has not promised any of us a rose garden! He has done something better than that, for through the propitiation of His Son, each of us has the opportunity of eternal life. God is clearly angered at what sin did to Adam and Eve. And this is gargantuan in the eyes of God, prodigious in cosmic events because his wrath escalates whenever God beholds sin and injustice in His world.

God's passion created us; God's final passion is for our holiness! But there is much deceit and wickedness in our world instigated by Satan and all of the evil spirits who roam through the world seeking the ruin of souls. Why is that? Because when Jesus Christ, the only Son of God was crucified, died and was buried, Jesus descended into Hell. Why? This is the moment when Jesus reaffirms his time has come and Satan's time is limited! Remember this, Satan and the evil angels that have fallen from Heaven, do not have redemption. Humanity possesses one of the greatest gifts from God, through Jesus Christ, redemption.

Each of us needs to safeguard that precious gift of redemption by following Jesus and not causing the wrath of God. So, what causes the wrath of God? We have the Bible, God's Word and Will to point the way. Jesus made visible what was invisible through his birth, ministry, crucifixion and death. Surely all sins provoke

God's wrath but there are mortal sins that insult and are abominations to Almighty God.

- Willful murder in all forms – suicide, euthanasia, abortion, killing of neighbors
- Sins of the Sodomites – sodomy under any other name is still sodomy
- The cry of the people oppressed
- The cry of the foreigner, the widow, the orphan
- Injustice to your neighbor
- Atheism – unbelief in God, an irreverence to God our Heavenly Father

All forms of sin and God's holiness just don't mix! God has a wrathful indignation, this is His passion to set things right in terms of sin, injustice and anything that afflicts the possibility of salvation. Holiness and sin cannot coexist. And thus, it was that God wants to set us on fire with the Holy Spirit and in holiness. Remember that God sent tongues of fire upon the Apostles and upon us at our Confirmation. And blessed be the God and Father of our Lord Jesus Christ, who in his great mercy gave us a new birth to a living hope through the resurrection of Jesus Christ from the dead, to an inheritance that is imperishable, undefiled, and unfading, kept in heaven for you who by the power of God are safeguarded through faith, to a salvation that is ready to be revealed in the final time. 1Pt1:3-5

Chapter 7

The Beast

God's Word speaks to us allegorically with extraordinary symbolism throughout the Bible just as Jesus teaches the truths through parables. Consequently, each of us in our daily prayer, worship and devotion seek to understand the truths that are being revealed by our Trinity God. God, our Father, through creation; God, the Son, through His Divine Mercy; God, the Holy Spirit, through the Gifts of the Holy Spirit bestow a special knowledge to believe, understanding to comprehend the omnipotence of God, wisdom to feel God's presence, counsel to seek the Almighty God, fear of the Lord, piety and fortitude so we persevere in faith.

When the Almighty God revealed to the Apostle John the vision of the end of the world as we know it, his primary purpose was to convey the impending apocalypse to the rest of the world. This is to prepare the way of the

A Believer

new enlightenment of the new heaven! This time with the full community of believers, the angels and the saints with Jesus Christ as our high priest; we give all glory and praise to God our Almighty Father in the new heaven of eternal light.

The "Beast," wow, what can I say about the beast in the book of Revelation? One picture is worth a thousand words. The beast with seven heads, ten horns and seven diadems. God with one picture summed up everything that needed to be said! The brilliance of His allegory sums up all of the 'questions' in our world and shows the crossroads of the end times.

The stark reality of life is our mortality and God's immortality with the gift of faith in-between, for as it states in the book of James 4:14, "You have no idea what your life will be like tomorrow. You are a puff of smoke that appears briefly and then disappears."

Now are you a believer or nonbeliever? Before you quickly answer that question, reflect on the parameters of life. A believer will accept and act on all the precepts set forth by God. Now what are those conditions set forth by our Heavenly Father. The Ten Commandments, the Beatitudes, the Golden Rule and the Sacraments by which Jesus has said, "Do this in memory of me." If we truly believe, then we accept and live by all of His precepts. We are not to be like the farmer who selectively picks only the choice fruit for market. To truly believe in God, all must accept all of His precepts. Our faith is an active one by doing. Plain and simple! And for those times that we have failed to live up to the scrutiny of our faith, then we should humble ourselves and go to confession. Penance is a soul cleansing sacrament that says to God, I am sorry for my sins, please forgive me and let me try again because I love you! Amen.

We have been prepared but, "until we all attain to the unity of the faith, and of the knowledge of the Son of God, to a mature person, to the measure of the stature which belongs to the fullness of Christ," we are incomplete! Eph 4:13

Christian re-birth happens as a onetime event, Baptism, which takes place in a moment of time. However, the process of sanctification, receiving the gifts of the Holy Spirit, will not cease, until we all come to the harmonious state of Christian unity, spiritual maturity, and Christlike conformity - when we see Him as He is.

From the beginning of time God has revealed himself, manifested through God the Creator, God the Son, through His Divine Mercy and God the Holy Spirit, the Sanctifier, through the Fire of tongues and gifts of the Holy Spirit.

It is difficult for humanity to comprehend an all-encompassing and all-embracing God. This is why God gave each of us a soul to listen to His Will, a heart to seek Him and a mind to embrace His word in the Bible. Then along with the enlightening gifts of the Holy Spirit, we begin our spiritual journey and through His

Divine Son, He shows us the way, truth and life. Beyond any of our comprehension, the process unravels through prayer, worship, devotion, Bible reading and almsgiving. Remember the words of St. Paul in Corinthians, chapter 14 to pursue love, but strive eagerly for the spiritual gifts, above all that you may prophesy; whoever prophesies builds up the church.

There is a clear distinction between prophecy and speaking in tongues. Prophecy is a message inspired by God. So, a prophet is one who receives God's message and transmits it to others or prophesies the message. A prophet is one who receives God's message and transmits it to others. Acts 3:18

Now comes speaking in tongues, or speaking directly to God. "For anyone who speaks in a tongue does not speak to men but to God. 1 Cor 14:2 Tongues is an intimate and direct line of communication with God through the Holy Spirit. When an individual is speaking in tongues, they are declaring the wonders of God and praising God at the same time.

God is our periscope in life to clear the way of our obstructed views of His Grace. He is the kaleidoscope of life to unveil the patterns in life of spirit, truth and mercy. He is our telescope in life to bring the distant Heaven into our soul. He is the microscope of life for the enlargement of faith, hope and love in our heart. God is our completeness in all things!

Humanity's Paradox

God's perspective on life is revealed in the very first chapters of Genesis and the Gospel of John. The End Times are revealed but not understood by the multitude in the last book of the Bible, Revelation. The significant words of God which make our lives rich and meaningful should come alive in our hearts and enamor us to follow our Lord, Jesus Christ.

In the beginning, when God created the heavens and the earth, the earth was a formless wasteland, and darkness covered the abyss, while a mighty wind swept over the waters. Then God said, "Let there be light, and there was light." Gn 1:1-3

Then in the prologue of the Gospel of John we read, In the beginning was the Word, and the Word was with God, and the Word was God. He was in the beginning with God. All things came to be through him, and without him nothing came to be. What came to be through him was life, and this life was the light of the human race; the light shines in the darkness, and the darkness has not overcome it. Jn 1:1-5

Then one can read in the prologue of Revelation, the revelation of Jesus Christ, which God gave to him, to show his servants what must happen soon. He made known by sending his angel to his servant John, who gives witness to the word of God and to the testimony of Jesus Christ by reporting what he saw. Blessed is the one who reads aloud and blessed are those who listen to this prophetic message and heed what is written in it, for the appointed time is near.

The darkness in life is Satan, and since the fall of the angels from heaven, has been attempting to overcome the light throughout the ages. The Will of God won't allow this and the end of time must come, so Christ can banish the darkness and establish the new eternal light forever.

Humanity has been prepared for this through God's word and even though the symbolism in Revelation is mindboggling, we are prepped by the Books of the Prophets, especially the words from the apocalypse of Isaiah about the devastation of the world and a remnant of humanity will be saved. The oracles and "Woes" of Jeremiah, "Faithfulness has disappeared; the word itself is banished from their speech." Jer7:28.

As to the why's this must happen, one only needs to look at Jer25:31

"To all who inhabit the earth to its very ends the uproar spreads; For the Lord has an indictment against the nations, he is to pass judgment upon all mankind; The godless shall be given to the sword, says the Lord."

The prophets lead us through the Will of God as Ezekiel, the very name means, "God Strengthens," describes his calling and encounter with God and four living creatures in a vision of the cherubim, the chariot, the Spirit and the four wheels showing the omnipresence, omniscience and omnipotence of God. As terrifying as this vision may be, it clearly revealed the majesty and glory of God.

Zechariah begins his book with a strong call to repent for Israel, which is also paramount for us today. Zec 1:1-6 The theme of repentance is developed more fully through the eight visions that he receives. All visions from God and especially those about the Messiah and his second Coming are paramount. But the known messages about salvation become apparent to the people of God as we pray, worship and meditate in devotion. To the ungodly, the message is oblivious.

This paves the way for the final prophesy of Revelation, through which more allegory depicts the message in kaleidoscope of the beast as seven heads, ten horns and seven diadems, representing the seven abominations, ten ideologies and seven conditions that alienate God and become the crossroads for the end. The final climatic wrath to end the reign of Satan and the tug of war between good and evil.

So, what are the seven abominations to God. We have to look at Proverbs 6:16-19 to find some answers.

1. A proud look – the pride of Satin
2. A lying tongue – Ananias and Sapphira
3. Hands that shed innocent blood – From Cain to Herod to the present age
4. Heart that plots wicked schemes – Nero to Hitler to Bin Laden to present

5. Feet that run towards evil – sex / drugs / crime / murder / apostasy
6. False witness that utters lies – just look at our courts and justice system
7. Whoever sows discord among brothers / blasphemy against God

In our present age today, one just needs to look at the random killings, adultery, abortions, robberies, sex trafficking, drugs, addictions, divorce and list never stops growing. God gave us the 10 Commandments and Jesus gave us the 8 Beatitudes to live a virtuous life. So, why, oh why don't we listen and obey His precepts? Time is running out! We are, as the people of Nineveh were, at a sackcloth moment but in our world, there is very little humility to get on our knees and not much reverence for God to say, "I am sorry for my sins," and to stop our transgressions.

So basically, what is an ideology you may ask? Well, a set of beliefs, principles and values adhered to by the multitude of society. Many of todays ideologies are contrary to God's ways. Remember the words of Jesus, "No one can serve two masters. Either you will hate the one and love the other, or you will be devoted to one and despise the other. You cannot serve both God and money." Mt 6:24

But this is also true about God and drugs, alcohol or any other addition, pornography, sexual immorality and habitually committing sin!

The problem with today and throughout ages past; the ideologies of society are not the ideals of God. God has made it very clear that love of God is ultimate, that his Son is the way, truth and the life to follow and utilize the gifts of the Holy Spirit to bear fruit and the reward is eternal life.

The warning from God for all; do not conform to the pattern of this world. Rm 12:1-2.

Let us scrutinize the Ideologies throughout the centuries. These ideologies in themselves are not immoral but the immoral leadership in our world that misconstrues their purpose. The first examples are of power structures.

- Anarchism rule by none: "I am an *anarchist* in politics and an impressionist in art as well as a symbolist in literature. Not that I understand what these terms mean, but I take them to be all merely synonyms of a pessimist." —Henry Brooks Adams (1838–1918)
- Democracy rule by the people: what happens when the majority lose their morals – example in mind abortion / injustice / no peaceable assembly – storming the capital

- Autocracy rule by one: From King Saul to Putin - big mistake
- Oligarchy rule by the few – China. Iran

Next would be political views.

- Communism – no more needs to be said – just look at Russia / China / North Korea
- Globalism
- Libertarianism
- Reactionary
- Totalitarianism
- Socialism
- Traditionalism
- Progressive

Next, the influence in our world of economic ideologies. There is nothing wrong with good sound economics to support subsistence to life as long as God's rule of one cannot serve two masters, "God or Money" is applied. Too many at the top of the pyramid have scraped the crème of the crop for themselves. Too many selfish embezzlements that rob pensions, the elderly and the needy.

Now we come to a sad truth that the work of the devil never ceases! The work of Satan is deceit and wickedness to destroy souls by any means. Religion is a pathway to lead us to God. The worship and practices set forth by God through His Holy Son and the Holy Spirit.

Divisiveness is a tool of Satan to rob many of the sacred practices in religion. We have one God, one divine Son and one Holy Spirit. How did we acquire so many religions?

Pinpointing precisely how many religions there are in the world today is next to impossible, although some estimate the number exceeds four thousand. The vast majority of those faiths are contained within a handful of major religious groups. The most widely recognized world religions are Christianity, Judaism, Islam, Buddhism, and Hinduism. The sad truth about many of these sects of religion is simply this, that they have missed the boat to lead the flock to God!

One God and one Golden Rule of "Love God with your whole heart, mind and soul and to love your neighbor as yourself." So, I ask, "What happened?" Why are there so many divisions of belief and why are there so many wars, persecutions and killings?

Finally, the seven conditions that bring the crossroads into conjunction to our final age.

- Abominations – Loathing of God's Laws and Truths
- Apostasies – Abandonment of religion
- Atheisms – Deny God and His Truths

A Believer

- Apathy – An Indifference, Obduracy to God's Truths – present example of abortion or preventing the development of life.
- Abandonments – Dereliction of the Gifts of Faith
- Abattoirs – Slaughterhouse of Animals, Humans – Life
- Aberrations – Deviation from God's Moral Standards – Ten Commandments, Eight Beatitudes & The Golden Rule

The leadership within our world also stands at the crossroads! Nations fail to live up to God's precepts. Throughout the ages, leadership should have made war obsolete. Our world lives at the precipice of nuclear holocaust, and the constant devastation by wars. At any one time there are better then fifteen conflicts in our world. Just look at the present state of affairs:

1. The United States has just exited from a 20-year war in Afghanistan.
2. Somali civil war in Africa.
3. Kashmir unrest in India.
4. War in Darfur Africa.
5. Civil War in Myanmar, Asia.
6. Conflict in Donbass, Ukraine.
7. Civil War in South Sudan, Africa.
8. Conflict in Peru, South America.

9. Conflict in Democratic Republic of Congo, Africa.
10. North Caucasus insurgency in Russia.
11. Civil War in West Papua, Asia.
12. Cabinda War in Angola, Africa.
13. War on terror in Egypt.
14. Hybrid War in Africa.
15. Military tensions in the South China Seas
16. Syrian Conflicts.
17. Nigerian Conflicts. (To name just a few)

The constant destruction of life through abortions adds to these atrocities. According to WHO, every year in the world there are an estimated **40-50 million** abortions. This corresponds to approximately 125,000 abortions per day. In the USA, where nearly half of pregnancies are unintended and four in 10 of these are terminated by abortion, there are over 3,000 abortions per day.

God is patient for us to turn to Him, but not forever! What about civil law vs God's law? We know that the laws are good if one uses it properly. We also know that the laws are made not for the righteous but for the lawbreakers and rebels, the ungodly and sinful, the unholy and irreligious, for those who kill their fathers and mothers, for murderers, for the sexually immoral, for those practicing homosexuality, for slave traders and liars and perjurers – and for whatever else is contrary to the

A Believer

sound doctrine that conforms to the gospel concerning the glory of the blessed God. 1Tim 1:8-11

Just take a stern look at the reality of life! We are told to enter by the narrow gate. For the gate is wide and the way is easy that leads to destruction, and those who enter by it are many. For the gate is narrow and the way is hard that leads to life, and those who find it are few." Matt. 7:13-14

The state of the affairs in our world are troublesome! We live in an immoral, godless society! Where is the Truth? The immoral bias of politics, journalism, internet media, and even our religion where there are too many false teachers have surpassed the licentiousness of Hollywood. We are on a crash course with Soul-corruption as well as Climate-change. Indeed, the Word of God is living and effective, sharper than any two-edged sword, penetrating even between soul and spirit, joints and marrow, and able to discern reflections and thoughts of the heart. No creature is concealed from God, but everything is naked and exposed to the eyes of him to whom we must render an account. Heb. 4:12-13

The answers to the crossroads of life lies in the inner life of the eschatological community as outlined to the end, the Parousia of Christ. The judgment draws near. The sober advice to, "humble yourselves under the mighty hand of God, that he may exalt you in due time. Cast all your worries upon him because he cares for you. Be sober and vigilant. Your opponent the devil is prowling around like a roaring lion looking for someone to devour. Resist him, steadfast in faith, knowing that your fellow believers throughout the world undergo the same sufferings." 1Pt 6:6-9

Chapter 8

The Alpha and Omega

"I am the Alpha and the Omega," says the Lord God, "the one who is and who was and who is to come, the Almighty." Rev 1:8

The reason for humanity, our purpose of existence is for God's glory. Our purpose with the gift of life is to praise and worship God and to accomplish His will. One needs to reflect and ask themselves, 'how many times does my will interfere with God's will?'

The preeminence of Christ, his person and hence also his work, is the image of the invisible God, the firstborn of all creation. For in him were created all things in heaven and on earth, the visible and the invisible, whether thrones or dominions or principalities or powers; all things were created through him and for him. He is before all things, and in him all things hold together. He is the head of the body, the church. He is the beginning, the firstborn from the dead, that in all things he himself might be preeminent. For in him all the fullness was pleased to dwell, and through him to reconcile all things for him, making peace by the blood of his cross, whether those on earth or those in heaven. Col 1:15-20

Before the beginning of time and the foundation of the world was formed, the angels were created in heaven to serve the Almighty God. The omnipotence of the Almighty God created nine choirs of angels for specific duties. The Seraphim, Cherubim and Thrones mediate upon the Person, wisdom and judgement of God. Then there are the Dominions, Powers and Virtues govern the forces of nature and the Universe as a whole. The last set of choirs are the Principalities, Archangels and Angels who are guardians.

First Sphere

- Seraphim
- Cherubim
- Thrones

Second Sphere

- Dominions
- Powers
- Virtues

Third Sphere

- Principalities
- Archangels
- Angels

Imagine the power of the Creator to create all things from the heavens to the universe and from the angels and all forms of life to humanity! To behold his omnipotence and glory and yet because of the choice of one angel, evil came into being!

Who has measured the waters in the hollow of his hand, or with the breadth of his hand marked off the heavens? Who has held the dust of the earth in a basket, or weighed the mountains on the scales and the hills in a balance? Is 40:12

One angel chose to sin against God by not wanting to be obedient to His Authority as Lord and Creator. But why did this angel, Lucifer, sin against God and dare to say, "Non serviam!" I will not serve? Because of Lucifer, a high-ranking cherub angel, through his arrogance of pride and envy wanted to rebel against God and took about a third of the angels with him in rebellion. This Lucifer became Satan, the devil which means accuser and adversary of God and through the devil's envy, death entered the world. Lucifer was prideful of his high status and beauty, but what he had was not enough for he wanted to be adored and worshiped like God.

The battlefronts were formed and seven angels stood between God and Satan; they led the rest of the loyal angels to cast Satan and his demons out of Heaven and into Hell. These seven defenders before God became known as Archangels.

Saint Michael the Archangel led the cohort of angels to defend our Almighty God and his name means, "Who is like unto God," and is patron of the Holy Eucharist. He is the Leader of the Armies of Heaven and he defends our souls against the infernal enemy when we call on him.

God was so moved by their heroic love that he elevated them to the position of highest heaven, standing eternally before the Throne of God to carry out God's Will.

"And from the throne, lightnings and voices and thunders went forth. And there were seven burning lamps before the throne, which are the seven spirits of God." Rev. 4:5

The good angels have made a permanent and indelible choice to submit to the love of God.

The fallen angels, now known as demons, are permanently rooted in sin. It is not possible for a devil to repent of his sins. This is "Lucifer's Paradox" and has become "Humanity's Paradox" for many! God is always in control. This was difficult for Lucifer and the fallen angels to fathom, and for many of humanity to accept. Those that do not believe that God is always in control of destiny are the scoffers.

A Believer

God is omniscient, all knowing, He is also absolute, Agape Love, the One that out of His Love creates. God Creates Heaven, the universe, the angels, life and finally humanity. God's preference is creation from his love to share. Destruction of any creation doesn't enter His omniscience. Because of the rebellion of the angels, comes the banishment from heaven. What follows in life is a string of rebellions due to Satan. First with Adam and Eve, Cain killing Abel, then the wickedness of humanity which causes the Great Flood. The immorality of humanity causes the banishment of Sodom and Gomorrah in brimstone and fire. The path of life is full of trials, tribulations and many agonies and the recipe for success in life is the essential element of choice. Each and every individual must choose to love God fully and follow His divine Son.

Thank God for the Cross of Christ, we lowly humans have redemption and a chance for eternal life, if we so choose to follow His Divine Son, Jesus Christ as the Way, Truth and Life to God, our Almighty Father.

"Let the wicked forsake their ways and the unrighteous their thoughts. Let them turn to the Lord, and he will have mercy on them, and to our God, for he will freely pardon. For my thoughts are not your thoughts, neither are your ways my ways," declares the Lord. "As the heavens are higher than the earth, so are my ways higher than your ways and my thoughts than your thoughts." Is. 55:7-9

Today the belligerent and arrogant flaunt their ways and do not see beyond their stuck-up noses and hardened hearts. Billionaires fund abortions, leaders deny upholding the truth, refugees are at a lost of where to turn, law, order and justice is at a loss, priest molest children, marriage is becoming a lost sacrament because divorce is rampart and licentiousness of the immoral grows day by day, hour by hour and minute by minute. Thoughts of the flesh are more ardent and prevalent then thoughts of the spirit! Television has become the hand-tool of the devil; too much nudity, violence, homosexuality, and defaming God's will. The truth of the matter is plain and simple; there is good and evil, our choices will lead us to either heaven or hell! Which choice is yours?

Doesn't anyone read the Bible anymore? Does anyone try to live up to God's truths? Does prayer, worship and devotion mean anything to those who received the gift of life from our Almighty God? Did Jesus Christ die in vain?

For when you were slaves of sin, you were free from righteousness. But what profit did you get then from the things of which you are now ashamed? For the end of those things is death. But now that you have been freed from sin and have become slaves of God, the benefit that you have leads to sanctification, and its end is eternal life. For the wages of sin is death, but the gift of God is eternal life in Christ Jesus our Lord. Rom 6:20-23

A Believer

The eternal way has been paved from the beginning of time since we have lessons from God about the past. "For if God did not spare the angels when they sinned, but condemned them to the chains of Tartarus and handed them over to be kept for judgement; and if he did not spare the ancient world, even though he preserved Noah, a herald of righteousness, together with seven others, when he brought a flood upon the godless world; and if he condemned the cities of Sodom and Gomorrah to destruction, reducing them to ashes, making them an example for the godless people of what is coming; and if he rescued Lot, a righteous man oppressed by the licentious conduct of unprincipled people, then the Lord knows how to rescue the devout from trial and to keep the unrighteous under punishment for the day of judgement, and especially those who follow the flesh with its depraved desire and show contempt for lordship. 2Pt2:4-10

There are also lessons to learn by the faith of the ancients. "Faith is the realization of what is hoped for and evidence of things not seen. By faith we understand that the universe was ordered by the word of God, so that what is visible came into being through the invisible. By faith Abel offered to God a sacrifice greater than Cain's. Through faith a trust in God is established that allowed Noah to build an ark, when no one else believed. That trust in faith is a continual sign for all peoples through the Patriarchs of Abraham, Isaac, Jacob and Joseph to do God's will and not their own.

That trust in God through faith caused Moses to lead the Hebrew people out of Egypt. From the rainbow in the sky, to the parting of the Red Sea, establishing His Covenant on Mt. Sinai and bringing the people to the promised land, God has always given awe inspiring signs that He is a real, loving Creator that cares for His people.

God has always pointed the way of his omnipotence through individuals of faith, the priests of the Levites, the patriarchs, the kings and the prophets. Through the long line of succession of kings, beginning with Saul, the kings that obeyed God flourished, and those kings that were disobedient to God, faltered. This points the way to our ultimate Priest, King, Prophet and Lord, Jesus Christ; He saves all who follow him through the blood of His Cross.

We are God's sanctified people through Christ, our Lord and Savior. Christians are the ones who are called to tell the world of God's goodness and grace. The Church, which is the Body of Christ, has been called to be God's witnesses to the whole world. As Christians come to Him, we discover that it was for the Church that Jesus prayed as He said, "And I consecrate Myself for them, so that they also may be consecrated in truth." Jn 17:19

For God so loved the world that he gave his one and only Son, that whoever believes in him shall not perish but have eternal life. For God did not send his Son into the world to condemn the world, but to save the world through him. Whoever believes in him is not condemned, but whoever does not believe stands condemned already because they have not believed in the name of God's one and only Son. Jn 3:16-18

Through the history of time, God revealed Himself as three Gods in one, the Father who is the Creator, the Son who is Divine Mercy and the Holy Spirit, who is the Sanctifier; the gift of life is a threefold purpose for us.

- Come to know God through His Divine Son
- Come to do His Will, utilizing the Gifts of the Holy Spirit
- Come to give Glory, Praise and Honor that God deserves and the fallen angels never learned

What can one say about our world today? Sin is rampant, deceit and wickedness are prevalent. We live in an ungodly world! From the beginning of time when out of God's love, He created us in His image; it was meant to be so beautiful. Before the foundation of the world, a fall in heaven took place and the tug of war between Good and Evil began. God sent His Son to be our way, truth and life but too many have turned away and don't follow and because of this our destiny has been set. Those that do believe and follow through the life-saving vessel of the church of baptism, prayer and worship have nothing to fear for God is with us!

Picture from Creative Commons

Therefore, since we have been justified by faith, we have peace with God through our Lord Jesus Christ, through whom we have gained access by faith to this grace in which we stand, and we boast in hope of the glory of God. Rm 5:1-2

If we confess our sins, he is faithful and just to forgive us our sins and to cleanse us from all unrighteousness. 1Jn 1:9

"Behold, I am coming soon. I bring with me the recompense I will give to each according to his deeds. I am the Alpha and the Omega, the first and the last, the beginning and the end." Rev 22:12-13

A Believer

For the age of BC has come and gone; the present age of AD is about to come to an end; the new age of EL, Eternal Light, is about to begin. Glory and praise to our God through Jesus Christ, our Lord. Alleluia, amen, again I say, AMEN!

Remember the words that Jesus Christ spoke to his disciples:

"There will be signs in the sun, the moon, and the stars, and on earth nations will be in dismay, perplexed by the roaring of the sea and the waves.

People will die of fright in anticipation of what is coming upon the world, for the powers of the heavens will be shaken. And then they shall see the Son of Man coming in a cloud with power and great glory. But when these signs begin to happen, stand erect and raise your heads because your redemption is at hand.

For that day will assault everyone who lives on the face of the earth. Be vigilant at all times and pray that you have the strength to escape the tribulations that are imminent and to stand before the Son of Man."

www.ingramcontent.com/pod-product-compliance
Lightning Source LLC
Chambersburg PA
CBHW021425070526
44577CB00001B/69